On the Vertical
By Ken Carlson

FAIR CHASE
IN NORTH AMERICA
BY CRAIG BODDINGTON

ILLUSTRATIONS BY KEN CARLSON

BOONE AND CROCKETT CLUB®
Missoula, Montana
2004

Fair Chase in North America

First Edition 2004

First Printing

Library of Congress Catalog Card Number: 2004104575
Paperback ISBN Number: 0-940864-47-9
Limited Edition Hard Cover ISBN Number: 0-940864-49-5
Published August 2004

Published in the United States of America
by the
Boone and Crockett Club
250 Station Drive
Missoula, MT 59801
406/542-1888
406/542-0784 (fax)
www.booneandcrockettclub.com

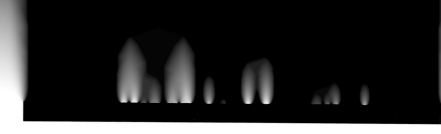

List of Illustrations

It has been more than 40 years since *Outdoor Life* published **The Big Game Animals of North America** by Jack O'Connor. It was about that time that my interest in big game hunting piqued and O'Connor's accounts of his personal experiences while hunting 20 different big game species, coupled with George C. Goodwin's accompanying natural histories provided the basis for a life-long love for wild places and the magnificent creatures that live there. I read and reread each of O'Connor's chapters and carefully studied Goodwin's natural histories, while I quietly dreamed of the day I could hunt for many of those same big game animals.

My first experiences with big game hunting began with mule deer on our family farm in the state of Washington. I began hunting mule deer about the same time I obtained O'Connor's book through the Outdoor Life Book Club. His accounts of mule deer hunting in Arizona provided new insights to what I already knew from hunting them on our farm with my father and brother. O'Connor's accounts of Arizona mule deer created an excitement within me as I thought about hunting big mule deer bucks elsewhere.

It was natural that O'Connor's book would serve as a basic reference for learning about one big game species after another over the years. From mule deer to elk to pronghorn to black bear and rocky mountain goat, O'Connor's writings served as a basis for further research. My first hunts for Alaska brown bear and Dall's sheep came 20 years after the publication of O'Connor's book. This past fall, more than 40 years after I obtained his book from the Outdoor Life Book Club, I went back and reread O'Connor's account on bighorn sheep in preparation for my hunt for a bighorn in Montana.

As time passed and I became successful in hunting different big game animals, my enjoyment of the hunting experience changed from the simple act of taking a borrowed rifle up on our "hill" after school or on a weekend to look for mule deer to a much more full appreciation for all aspects of the hunt. Subtle aspects of the hunt such as the chatter of the Douglas squirrel, the call of the nuthatch, the hollow clanking of the bells on my horses in elk camp or the fragrance of a fir thicket on a north slope in Northern Idaho created an excitement much greater than a simple hike up on the "hill" in hopes of seeing a deer. The nature of my enjoyment for hunting and exploring new, wild, and remote places fostered my active participation in all aspects of the hunt. It was not long before I was backpacking into rough country in far away places scouting new areas and learning the habits of more and more big game species. Soon, I understood the value of owning one's own saddle and pack stock. This led to learning to pack and ride, as well as a myriad of other associated skills required for safe and successful hunting in the backcountry on my own. Soon my collateral interests, experiences, and skills related to hunting were as important to me as was the hunting experience itself. My interest in hunting and outdoor literature, rifles, shotguns, ballistics, outdoor photography, map reading, horses, dogs, and the history of our wildlife cultural heritage soon became so woven into my life that they became a part of my identity.

Given this history, it seemed only natural that I would become acquainted with the Boone and Crockett Club and its Records of North American Big Game program. My first interest in the Club came through the "records" program, but it was not long before my interest in the Club's publications surpassed my interest in records. It was in the fall of 1992 when Club President, Steve Adams, asked me to assume the responsibilities for the Club's Associates Program and the *Associates' Newsletter*.

The first task was to develop an appropriate means of communicating the Club's mission, visions, and programs to the Club's membership. This was accomplished by hiring Julie Tripp (Houk) to provide oversight for the layout and design of the *Associates' Newsletter*. Soon after we hired Julie, our Associates provided ideas for a more formal name for the newsletter. *Fair Chase* was selected as the title for the new official publication of the Boone and Crockett Club from among 46 different titles proposed by Boone and Crockett Associates. Associates Chris Keenum of Hartsell, Alabama, and Don Moody of Gainesville, Texas both submitted the title *Fair Chase*.

With a new title and a lead staff person to oversee this new publication, we launched *Fair Chase* magazine with the Winter 1994 issue. The first two issues were well received by our Associates, but we needed a more well-defined editorial policy and a focal point for the magazine. With an eye to this venture, the influence of Jack O'Connor's writings and **The Big Game**

INTRODUCTION

Animals of North America had upon me as an eager, young hunter stood out in my mind as I searched for an overarching plan for the series of articles that would become the centerpiece of *Fair Chase*. When my friend, Biff Mac Collum of Phoenix, Arizona, reminded me of his keen interest in O'Connor's articles on each of the big game species in this book, the project's format became clear in my mind. Each of the issues of *Fair Chase* over the next four years would feature a species of North American big game on the cover and an article about that species by Craig Boddington. Early issues also contained an article about the natural history of the species written by Dr. Philip L. Wright.

It was fitting that Craig write these lead articles for he and Jack O'Connor were past hunting editors for *Peterson's HUNTING*. Craig was a professional member of the Boone and Crockett Club and had first-hand experience hunting and writing about our North American big game. His writing and field experience made Craig eminently qualified for this assignment. As with O'Connor, I had read most of Boddington's articles on North American big game and had an appreciation for the knowledge and expertise evident in his writing. By this time in my life, I too had acquired first-hand experience hunting many of the different North American big game species and found that my experiences afield were consistent with Boddington's work. A telephone call to Craig was all it took to seal the deal and for the next four years his articles served as the centerpiece for *Fair Chase* magazine.

When Craig concluded his last article in the North American big game series in the summer of 1998 we talked of publishing all of the articles at a later date in one combined volume. I actually had this vision in mind when we started the series and was very pleased when Craig agreed to work with the Boone and Crockett Club in publishing **Fair Chase in North America**.

When *Outdoor Life* published **The Big Game Animals of North America** in 1961, our world was quite different from what it is today. Today, our population has shifted to be overwhelmingly urban. As a result, generations of Americans have little or no contact with the outdoors or wildlife. Modern societal norms have influenced the motivations and attitudes related to hunting. In today's fast-paced society, fewer hunters have the time to seek out new hunting territories and learn the biology and behavior of their quarry. Time seems to be short and the "endless day" that typifies many of our lives has a great deal to do with where we hunt, when we hunt, and how we hunt.

By focusing on the "Fair Chase" hunting tradition as the common denominator, the Boone and Crockett Club has harnessed the passion of generations of hunters for the conservation of wildlife and its habitat for the common good of the American people. This passion, for over a century of conservation in North America, has led to the protection of Yellowstone, Glacier, and Denali National Parks; the foundation of the National Forest Service, National Park Service, and National Wildlife Refuge; the passing of the Pittman-Robertson and Lacey Acts, and the establishment of the Federal Duck Stamp Program. The North American Model of Wildlife Conservation and much of our nation's conservation infrastructure and heritage can be traced back, directly or indirectly, to the Boone and Crockett Club.

A major part of the Club's conservation legacy lies in having defined and promoted the "rules of the chase" for hunting North American big game, which provided the foundation for hunter ethics throughout North America and, to some extent, the world. Adherence to Fair Chase ethics have defined the requirements for inclusion of big game trophies in the Boone and Crockett Club's North American Big Game Records Program — the program by which all other trophy recognition programs are measured.

Fair Chase in North America incorporates the Boone and Crockett Club's Fair Chase traditions and presents them in the context of the modern hunter in today's society. Craig Boddington has accomplished a masterful work in sharing his experiences afield in a manner that is enjoyable to read while providing insight into hunting techniques and the habits and traits of our North America big game species.

The Boone and Crockett Club is indebted to Craig Boddington for his many contributions to the Club as a professional member. After reading ***Fair Chase in North America***, we hope you will share our enthusiasm.

BY GEORGE A. BETTAS, ED.D.
Executive Director
Boone and Crockett Club

CHAPTER ONE ▪ CARIBOU
Nomads of the North

CARIBOU! IT'S FEAST OR FAMINE WHEN YOU HUNT THE NOMADS OF THE NORTH – BUT BEING THERE IS AT LEAST HALF THE FUN!

I'll never forget the first caribou I ever saw. It was nearly 30 years ago now, and I was on a mixed-bag hunt in British Columbia — back when such hunts, though hardly commonplace, were laughably affordable by today's standards.

We were looking for Stone's sheep, my Indian guide and I, working our way up a knife-edged ridge in the Cassiars. There were some sheep, all right, far away below a distant snow pack. Much closer on an intervening ridge, the twin to the one we were on, a set of massive antlers floated above the skyline. He was a World's Record for sure, with double shovels and tall beams and good top points. And even if he wasn't a World's Record, he was all the caribou I needed to see. He was also all the caribou my guide needed to show me.

When those floating antlers dropped out of sight, we jumped on our horses and followed the contour around to the next ridge. We dismounted and worked our way down the spine, finding the caribou on about the third little bench. He was bedded in a little depression, and when he stood I shot him very carefully in the shoulder.

No, he was not a World's Record. In fact, he was not really a very good caribou. What size he had was greatly exaggerated by the heavy August velvet. However, it was some years before I realized that, and it's never made any difference anyway. He was my first caribou, and like all firsts, he was and is very special.

Since then I've been fortunate to have hunted caribou in lots of places, from Newfoundland to Quebec to Northwest Territories and on to the Yukon and Alaska. I kind of like them, but perhaps not for the most obvious reasons. They are beautiful with those wonderful antlers unexcelled in the deer kingdom and, as winter approaches, the snow-white flowing mane. But I can't say they match the majesty of a fine elk or the breathtaking wonder of a big ram. I certainly can't rate them high in the challenge department. How shall I say this kindly? In terms of interaction with hunters, caribou are not rocket scientists. Even in the venison department, they don't quite compare with our other antlered species. (This was brought home to me one time when I spent four days in a tent waiting for a plane with nothing but caribou — no ketchup, no salt!)

And yet there's a special charm about being in caribou country in the early fall, with the low scrub turning golden and crimson and the ptarmigan shifting to white. The landscape is completely empty, horizon to horizon. And yet caribou must be there, perhaps in a hidden fold — or perhaps, as you watch, a great herd will march over the far horizon.

That actually happens, and the mere possibility of seeing the spectacle of the caribou migration is another thing that brings many of us to caribou country. However, it doesn't happen often. That's not true. It happens once every autumn at every point along each caribou herd's migration route. The problem lies in being at that point at that time. And there's the big rub with caribou hunting.

Few hunts in North America can be as feast or famine as caribou hunting. If they're there, they're really there, and in numbers that literally march to the horizon, one group after another. If they're not there, well . . .

Actually, it isn't as grim as that. The peak of the migration, especially with some of the larger regional herds, is a fabulous sight. But it isn't one great press of animals. Rather, it's group after group that will be many days in the passing. First a trickle, then a flood, and finally a few stragglers — sometimes the largest bulls of all.

Across North America I suppose I have hunted caribou maybe 15 times. Just twice have I really been in exactly the right place at exactly the right time. The first time was on the barrens of Northwest Territories, when caribou hunting was first opening and before anyone had thought of creating our Central Canada barren ground caribou category. I went in with some Indians, whose goal was to secure their winter meat. We pitched camp by a small lake with a vast flat to our north and, beyond that, a long,

Very few caribou "have it all." This barren ground caribou, taken in the Yukon, has exceptional tops and I like him, but I knew all along he had fairly weak shovels and bez formations.

low ridge. The first couple of days were uneventful, with just a small scattering of caribou passing through and no mature bulls at all. Then the floodgates opened and the caribou marched past. Each hour would bring a new herd skylined on that distant ridge. The next hour would bring them within a few hundred yards of our tent, and by then a fresh herd would be skylined on the ridge. It went on for days and was still happening when we left.

The second time was in the fall of 2001, just a few days before our world changed on September 11th. I was on a semi-guided hunt southwest of Kujuuaq (formerly Fort Chimo), where the burgeoning Leaf River herd comes through. The first couple of days there were what I'd describe as "some caribou" percolating around camp — plenty enough to see and hunt, but not in great numbers and really not migrating. I know this because I saw the same distinctive bulls in different places on different days. I took a nice bull early on, and most of the hunters in camp filled one or both tags in the first three or four days.

With just two days left in the hunt the wind changed, and we woke up to the spectacle of the genuine migration! Caribou in groups small and large, with many big bulls, marched around our camp on both ends of the lake for the next two days. Gunmaker Lex Webernick, who had held out, took two spectacular caribou. I had one tag left and took one of my very best bulls. Those of us who had filled out too quickly, well, all they could do was watch and drool!

Remember, though, this is just two occasions out of a number of caribou hunts across the North Country. The other extreme was that mountain caribou I mentioned earlier. That was the only caribou I saw that trip, and Dad never saw one at all. So I suppose that bull wasn't all that bad after all!

The rest of my caribou hunts have been somewhere in between, ranging from fairly tough to fairly plentiful, but usually plenty of caribou to look at. A fairly tough one was a hunt I made in Quebec in 1983, out of Schefferville. Caribou fanatics will almost certainly remember that as the year the great George River herd changed their migration route. Mostly we looked at empty landscape. Lots of empty landscape. This was a camp that had been on the migration route for years — easy hunting, big bulls, 100 percent success. The outfitter was spoiled. The guides were spoiled. The hunters came expecting to be spoiled. That year the only thing that was spoiled was expectations of an easy hunt!

Actually, there were a few caribou around. Rather than what a typical Quebec caribou hunt had been for years, it was more like most other typical North American hunts. But success was possible if you were willing to hunt hard. The guides were and the outfitter certainly was. Surprisingly, a few of the hunters were not. They went home without caribou. The rest of us pitched in and walked our tails off, and we scratched out some pretty fair caribou.

Most typical, perhaps, was the first trip I made to Newfoundland — not too easy, but not too tough. After a couple of days of seeing little close by camp my crew determined the caribou must be hung up on a big plateau a few miles away. That's common, by the way, for caribou herds to stop for a day or a week — especially with caribou that migrate only short distances, if at all. That includes most woodland and mountain caribou herds that I'm aware of.

So, since the caribou clearly weren't coming to us, we went to them. We left camp hours before dawn, and it was long after dark when we got back, but we reached the caribou right on schedule, shortly before midday — and indeed there were plenty of them. I like Newfoundland. I've hunted there twice more since, and probably will return. However, that was the day I shot my best woodland caribou. He had it all — good mass, good shovels, good bez, and lots of points. Even at that I shot much too quickly. While we field-dressed my bull, a herd with two much larger caribou fed over the hill to us!

The good news is that the migration isn't a sudden event, nor is it a flash flood that comes with no warning and quickly abates. In Quebec last year the caribou around camp were probably the advance guard, with the bulk hanging back somewhere over the horizon and not moving much . . . until the wind changed and here they came. A few years ago Randy Brooks and I went on another semi-guided hunt in Quebec, but that time we went at the tail end of the season, the last week in September.

This camp had enjoyed a spectacular season, but by the time we got there the migration had almost passed, with just a few tail-end Charlies coming through. We hiked and we glassed, and we shivered endlessly at crossings. On the first day I passed up a pretty good bull, figuring we would see better, but as the days passed we saw fewer and fewer caribou. Persistence counts, so we stayed at it. Usually there will be some good bulls trailing the main migration, and so it was. On the next to the last day, Randy and I both took very fine caribou. Actually, he shot two nice caribou, and I took a real dandy. On the last day, as I recall, we saw no bulls at all!

All this may sound like caribou hunting is routinely successful. It is . . . if you go to the right place and hunt caribou. Only once have I been altogether in the wrong place. That was on an unguided caribou hunt in 1975, and while the country was beautiful, the caribou just weren't there yet. Even so, I have quite a collection of unused caribou tags. Mostly these remained unused because I attempted to hunt caribou as an adjunct to some other primary quarry. Usually that doesn't work. Few North American areas are really prime for more than one species at the same time. Or there isn't time after the primary animal is taken.

For instance, I shot a fabulous moose during the Alaska Peninsula's short moose season. Although this area also produces some of the finest caribou, late September was a bit early for the main herds to come out of the mountains that year. Also on the Peninsula and at the right time of year, I got a wonderful brown bear, but although there were plenty of good caribou around, there just wasn't time remaining to hunt them. Sometimes, even if the caribou are there, the circumstances just aren't right.

I had both a caribou tag and a Dall's sheep tag on a backpack hunt into the Mackenzie Mountains a couple of years ago. I was absolutely shocked at some of the beautiful mountain caribou I saw almost daily, but to shoot a caribou would have ended the sheep hunt, at least until we got the meat and horns packed out of the mountains. So I kept looking at wonderful caribou while we hunted sheep — and of course there was no time remaining when we finally got the ram!

My Yukon hunt in '99 was just the opposite. I got a great ram early on and had plenty of time to hunt caribou, my choice for my second animal on what was essentially a two-species hunt. But it was September and most of the caribou had already moved out of the mountains. We didn't see many, but

TOP: A really superb Quebec-Labrador caribou, taken in September 2001 from the fast-growing Leaf River herd. This one has excellent length and mass, great tops, and spectacular bezes; his only real problem is that he has just one shovel.
BOTTOM: This bull was one of the first caribou taken by a non-resident on the barrens of Northwest Territories. We now call them Central Canada barren ground caribou.

we stuck with it for several days and I took a really neat bull with exceptional top points.

The lesson is that caribou hunting is extremely successful, but it's at its best when you hunt caribou exclusively and seriously. If you do that, you're unlikely to bring home unfilled tags. In fact, you have a very good chance of bringing home a monster. You always have to be at the right place at the right time, but given proper planning and a bit of luck, record-class specimens of each of our five caribou varieties remain very possible prizes.

Among the hard parts are knowing a good caribou when you see him... and making a sound judgment as to how likely you are to see a better one. As I've said, I've made some mistakes in the latter area. If caribou are on the move you can't put them in the bank; the chances of seeing a particular bull again are very unlikely. So you have to make your best judgment based on the situation. If this is early in the hunt it's a tough call because you may not yet know exactly what's going on. As to the former, well, caribou racks are very hard to judge because there are so many features to look at.

It's easy to get carried away by double shovels, huge bez formations, and long top points. The trick is to take your time and evaluate the whole rack. No caribou are perfect, so you're looking for a blend of all these characteristics, plus long beams, and, optimally, decent back points. And of course you have to keep in mind exactly which caribou you're looking at!

The five varieties of caribou recognized by the Boone and Crockett Club are a reflection of regional antler differences recognized by hunters more than actual subspecies recognized by biologists. Indeed most biologists do agree on five subspecies of caribou currently extant in North America, plus an extinct subspecies that used to live in the Queen Charlotte Islands. But the biologists' five subspecies and the hunters' five classifications are not the same!

Biologists, for instance, maintain that all the caribou across southern Canada, from Newfoundland through Quebec and Labrador, across northern Ontario and all the way west to northern B.C., southern Yukon, and the Mackenzies are

TOP: Packing out the cape and horns of a really good Quebec-Labrador caribou. This bull was taken at the tail end of the migration.
BOTTOM: Although not a record-class bull, this is a very typical Quebec-Labrador caribou with a very wide spread, broad shovel, and big, palmated bez formations.

Rangifer tarandus caribou, the woodland caribou. To this day Northwest Territories licenses the caribou in the Mackenzies as woodland caribou. Based on both size differences and regional antler configurations hunters have long separated *R. t. caribou* into three classifications: Mountain caribou in British Columbia, southern Yukon, and the MacKenzie District of Northwest Territories; Quebec-Labrador caribou in northern Quebec and Labrador; and woodland caribou in Newfoundland and on west to the timbered portions of the prairie provinces.

Rangifer tarandus granti stands alone as the large barren ground caribou of Alaska and northern Yukon, while *R. t. groenlandicus* is now properly recognized as the slightly smaller Central Canada barren ground caribou. Those are hunters' five classifications, leaving the small Peary caribou of Canada's offshore islands (*R. t. pearyi*) currently unrecognized, likewise the *ergogroenlandicus* of southern Greenland. These have not been recognized by B&C because of possible hybridization with mainland caribou, and concerns over small numbers that may not support hunting pressure.

If you put an average to very good caribou mount of each of the five on a wall, very few hunters could readily identify its classification. There are significant regional antler trends, but they're trends only. One of the neat things about caribou — and one of the frustrations in judging them — is that few caribou short of the current World's Records have everything all in one place! Here's my spin on our five caribou, and some of the best places to hunt them.

Woodland Caribou: Although fairly large in the body, woodland caribou are our smallest-racked caribou. Oddly, double shovels are very common, as are strong bez formations. Numerous points are also common, but main beams tend to be quite short, and I've found it very difficult to find woodland caribou with good (sometimes any) top points. Newfoundland is just about the only place nonresidents can hunt woodland caribou, and certainly is the best place. Newfoundland has lots of woodland caribou and plenty of good ones. This island province also has plenty of very fine, well-organized outfitters, and prices are very reasonable. However, few Newfoundland outfitters are really geared for trophy hunting. The best course is to book a caribou hunt,

A caribou can usually be packed out in two loads — if you're in good shape. Unlike moose, they aren't so large that you need to think carefully about where you are before you take the shot.

not the typical moose-caribou combination, and make sure your outfitter understands you want to look for the best caribou possible in the time available to hunt.

Mountain Caribou: Mountain caribou at their best have tall racks with fabulous top formations, often palmated, but shovels and bez are usually not strong. In years gone by northern B.C. was the place, but this caribou herd has dropped significantly in recent years for reasons that seem unclear to local biologists. The Spatsizi Plateau and adjacent areas are the best opportunity in B.C. Southern Yukon remains pretty good, but these days the best mountain caribou hunting is found in Northwest Territories' Mackenzie Mountains. In the past most caribou were taken as an addition to sheep hunting, which is a poor way to hunt caribou. These days a few of the MacKenzie outfitters are now offering later caribou or moose-caribou hunts, after the caribou come down into the valleys. That's a good opportunity for very fine bulls.

Quebec-Labrador Caribou: These caribou, at their best, tend to be very wide, relatively thin-beamed, but with broad, palmated bez and shovel formations. Labrador, where the World's Record was taken, is still relatively unhunted. Most camps are out of Kujuuaq or Schefferville in northern Quebec. The Schefferville camps are mostly hunting the George River herd, which, although still large, has been in decline for several years. Out of Kujuuaq the hunting is for the Leaf River herd, currently growing by leaps and bounds and, by some estimates, now approaching a million animals. These days I think the larger Leaf River herd offers the best odds, but the problem with northern Quebec is that the hunting is from established camps, comfortable, but based on historic herd movement. That can change, and in some years even the best camps can be left high and dry.

Central Canada Barren Ground Caribou: At their best, Central Canada caribou have it all — good shovels, reasonable bez, back points, long beams, multi-tined tops. They just don't quite have what Alaskan caribou have! These are the caribou of Northwest Territories' barrens and the herd is still expanding. Most of the better caribou have come from Mackay Lake and Courageous Lake regions, but this country is still being opened up. This is our newest caribou classification, and I suspect we'll see the current minimum of 345 revised upward as we learn how big these caribou can really become. Right now Central Canada barren ground caribou is one of the easier animals to obtain a record-class specimen of.

Barren Ground Caribou: These are our largest-racked caribou, characterized by long main beams in a "C" configuration, with, at their best, a little bit of everything: broad shovels; long, strong bez formations; back points; and tall top points. Alaska is the place, but Alaska is a very big place. A good bet remains with the rapidly-expanding Mulchatna herd in west-central Alaska. The Peninsula herd remains a very fine trophy producer, and some of the caribou coming from the western approaches to the Brooks Range are surprisingly outstanding.

Relatively few of us will want to hunt all five of our caribou. Of those of us who have, fewer still can say that we've found specimens of each that really exemplify the classification. I certainly haven't! The wonderful thing is that, wherever you hunt them, caribou hunting is quite similar and a whole lot of fun. Lots of glassing, lots of walking, lots of stalking — and, if conditions are even close to right, lots of game to be seen. As a game animal I don't put caribou on a par with many other North American species, but they sure are fun to hunt!

CHAPTER TWO ▪ BIGHORN
Magnificent Bighorn Sheep

THANKS TO SOME OF THE MOST INTENSIVE AND MOST EFFECTIVE CONSERVATION EFFORTS THIS PLANET HAS SEEN OUR BIGHORNS ARE COMING BACK — AND A GREAT RAM IS TODAY A POSSIBLE PRIZE.

It was nearly dark when we spotted the ram. We had made a cold November camp beside long-frozen Spirit Lake, and he was miles away, all the way up on top of a charming place known as Froze To Death Plateau — one of the most apt place names I've ever seen. Although Montana is a mountainous state, there are no really high peaks there. Froze To Death is as high as it gets at 11,000 feet and a bunch of change. In November in a year that brought an early winter that's very high indeed.

The ram was alone, and he was on a slide of jumbled shale right on the edge of the plateau where it dropped off into our valley. Had he not been skylined we would never have seen him at so great a distance. But see him we did, and we watched him bed right there in the shale.

We moved on him at three o'clock in the morning, following a steep and snow-drifted trail that led to the top of the plateau. It was cold in the valley, but it was brutal as we topped out in the pre-dawn chill. A freezing wind ripped at us, and although our timing was close we had to huddle in the lee of a boulder and shiver until it grew light enough to proceed.

I was with Jack Atcheson Jr., one of the great sheep hunters of our time and one of few people to achieve consistent success in Montana's "Unlimited Permit" areas, one of which we were hunting. Jack never breathed hard on the climb, nor did he shiver in the wind. I did lots of both.

From below, with spotting scope turned up all the way, the ram had appeared exceptionally legal — not a "book" ram, but a very fine mature specimen, especially from the rugged unlimited zones where sheep rarely grow the best horns. He also appeared to be alone. Later we would conclude that he was the only sheep on top of Froze To Death — and what in the heck he was doing, all the way up there in the rocks that late in the year, I have no idea. He hadn't moved in the 12 hours since we last saw him, and therefore he surprised us as much as we surprised him.

He jumped up and I dropped down across a rock and got the cross hairs on him. He was 250 yards away, and the crosswind was a good 30 miles per hour. It was a difficult shot at best, but it was a very possible shot, and it wasn't really a great surprise. We'd thought we might find him somewhere on that shale slope, and I'd been thinking about the wind and what to do about it ever since I'd first felt its force. The problem was that I didn't shoot.

My explanation — to Jack then, to you now, and to myself over the last few years — was that I first looked at the horns to make sure he was legal. And in that split second he turned and was gone over an unseen lip. When he reappeared he was well past 400 yards and running like the hounds of hell were after him. We watched him cross a boulder-strewn valley, climb the far ridge, and vanish over Froze To Death the best part of a mile away. He was still running like I never knew a wild sheep could run.

We tracked him, but he gave us the slip in some boulders. We never saw him again that day. We did see him again two days later, when we were at the bottom of the valley once again and we spotted him slipping through a high saddle. So we climbed Froze To Death once more. However, that brief glimpse was the last we saw of him. Soon it was time to pack out and make sure the area's quota hadn't been filled. And, to be perfectly honest, I'd had my fill of Froze To Death Plateau.

In the few years that have passed since then I've relived those seconds over and over again. I had wanted a bighorn most of my life, and at that time I'd been rejected in the permit drawings for about 15 years. It's an easy one to second guess. I had the shot, I knew what to do about the wind, but I didn't shoot. Did I really check the horns to make sure he was the right ram? And if I did, was that the right thing to do? Or, as I'm sure Jack suspects, but was too much a gentleman to voice, did I freeze up? I wish I knew.

Jack Atcheson, Jr., in Montana's "unlimited permit" bighorn country. This is unfinished business. I've tried a couple of times, but luck hasn't smiled. It's high and steep, but sheep are there. I will keep trying.

Time passed and I kept applying. Nothing happened, of course. I'd been unsuccessful for so long that the ritual of permit applications simply gave me a reverse savings account for fall hunting! Secretly I figured I deserved the rejection, for I'd had a chance, but had blown it, whether for the right reasons or not. Jack and I talked about trying the unlimited areas again, but somehow didn't quite get it put together. And by then you had to make your decision at application time between a permit area and an unlimited area — so I stuck with the permit draws with no real anticipation of it happening. Not only Montana, of course. I've been pretty consistent in Wyoming, and in some years I've put it for New Mexico, Idaho, and of course I started in Colorado as soon as non-resident permits were authorized. On the desert side, I don't think I've missed many years in Arizona and Nevada, and I've applied in Utah when I could scrape up the money.

I could have booked a bighorn hunt in Alberta or British Columbia. My excuse has been that I can't afford it, but that's really just an excuse. I manage to get to Africa frequently enough that I suppose I could have booked a bighorn hunt if I wanted to badly enough. However, time passed and I stuck with the permit draws almost as a ritual — not because I really believed it might someday work.

In 1993 U.S. Outfitters' George Taulman started his computerized tag application service, and I signed up. I seriously doubted George knew more about the application process than I did after 20 years, but it sure made life simpler.

It wasn't George who called in the spring of '94 to tell me I'd drawn the Montana tag. It was Jack Atcheson Jr., who'd just gotten the printout from the game department. Quite honestly, and I hate to admit this, I didn't even remember George had put me in for Montana. But he did and I drew. Not in just any area, but in the portion of area 340 west of I-15, the Pioneer Mountains. This is one of those golden areas that has been producing some of the finest rams in North America. It depends on

TOP: In Wyoming, outfitter Ron Dube sets up for a serious glassing session for bighorns. While you might see sheep at almost any level, the most likely is sagebrush pockets right at timberline, where sheep will feed in the mornings and evenings.
BOTTOM: I took this ram in Montana's Area 340, one of several particularly good trophy ram units. Such permits are very hard to draw, but well worth applying for! The rifle is a Dakota Model 76 in .270 caliber.

who you talk to as to whether Rock Creek, the Butte Highlands, or the Pioneers are the best — they're all good.

Truth is this hunt was a stark contrast to my experiences in the unlimited permit zones. You might even say it was anti-climactic. It was in all ways a grand experience. Atcheson went with me to help out, and we saw rams, and lots of them, every morning and every afternoon. In fact, we saw about 90 rams. We climbed no mountains, although we climbed a few hills. My father, who at 72 had never seen a wild sheep, also came along to help. He saw a good 50 rams, and he climbed no hills at all. In other words, it was not a sheep hunt as legend has sheep hunts to be. It was not a sheep hunt as my hunts for Stone's and Dall's sheep have been, but it was truly fabulous — and it was quite possibly akin to the sheep hunting our forefathers might have known.

After that hunt I figured I'd had my bighorn luck. Not quite. In '98 I drew a Wyoming permit in the high country south of Cody and east Yellowstone. This was an altogether different experience. I hunted with old friend and veteran outfitter Ron Dube, who has outfitted in the Cody area for many years. In other words, the hunt would be on his home turf. I told him from the start that I had no expectation of taking a bigger ram than I'd gotten in Montana four years earlier. I wanted a mature, grown-up bighorn, but that was as picky as I'd be. With this in mind Ron figured we'd have a ram in five or six days. I figured a week and planned for ten days to be sure.

We had a wonderful hunt on horseback in some of North America's prettiest country. We started from a comfortable cabin Ron uses for late deer hunts, later spiking out into some really spectacular country. We saw sheep every day, and over time I think we saw something like 14 legal rams, but by the evening of the ninth day we had yet to see a genuinely mature ram. Figuring a change was needed, we packed up and spent that night at Ron's house, trailering horses to a trailhead west of Cody the next morning.

We rode up into the high country and tied the horses, sepa-rating to head up to different overlooks. My spot looked easy enough to reach, but it was a nightmare. I clawed my way up through snowy timber, then scared the hell out of myself scram-bling across a frozen chute. Finally I broke out of the timber, then plowed through crusted drifts toward the saddle we'd marked as my vantage point. I was almost to the top when, faintly, I heard Ron Dube's shrill whistle. He'd spotted something!

It took me forever to glass him up on the opposite slope, but when I finally got the binoculars on him he was gesturing wildly toward the horses. I bailed off the ridge and headed for the bottom, through the timber, across that scary chute, and down through more timber. Ron already had the horses when I spilled out on the trail, and he met me with a grin. The name of his outfit is "Ron Dube's Wilderness Adventures." He said, "The hunting phase of this Ron Dube wilderness adventure is now concluded. The harvesting phase has just begun."

He had spotted the unlikely combination of two mature rams and one ewe in a little sagebrush patch far below. We had maybe three hours of daylight left and a long distance to ride. It was possible, but we needed a bit of luck. We didn't get it, not that night. We got into the general area ahead of sunset, but up close the ground looked a lot different. As dark fell we concluded the sheep had to be on one of three or four finger ridges, but by then we were out of time. We pulled well back into the timber, got a fire going, and spent a long, cold night huddled in damp horse blankets.

In the morning things went just like clockwork. We started down one ridge and found the sheep bedded on the next ridge, across a little cut. One ram and the ewe were mostly hidden by vegetation, but the second ram was in the clear, lying facing away on a little uphill slope. The distance was a bit less than 275 yards. I had the shot, and a steady position to make it from. However, bedded animals are tricky, and the light breeze was in our favor. I decided to wait, and Ron agreed. It was endless and it was agonizing, but eventually the ram stood and I shot him. He was exactly what I'd wanted, a mature, grown-up bighorn. He was a hard-won prize, and I value him every bit as much as the much larger Montana ram!

Ovis canadensis, the bighorn sheep, is not really a creature of the high mountains. In the days of pre-European man he certainly existed in the high country, but perhaps much like the mule deer he was equally, and perhaps more so, a creature of the breaks and foothills. Custer hunted him on his Black Hills expedition a year before his fateful hunting trip along the Little Big Horn — and there's a reason for the name of that river. Theodore Roosevelt hunted him in the Black Hills as well. Unfortunately wild sheep, especially in the foothills and badlands regions, were extremely vulnerable to the excessive hunting of the last century. Worse, all wild sheep are extremely vulnerable to domestic animal diseases. By the early years of around your ears. That makes things a bit tricky, and almost certainly prevents these areas from reaching their hunting potential. I've been in there, and I reckon if you could spend three weeks at it, the hunting would be every bit as good as some of the famed Canadian bighorn grounds. However, good or bad, I love the concept that anybody can still go sheep hunting if he or she is tough enough. I hope Montana sticks with the program!

My uncle, Art Popham, whose work has also graced Boone and Crockett Club's magazine, was one of the early "grand slammers." In the 1930s, desert sheep hunting in Mexico was not a big problem. Bighorns were no problem in the '30s and '40s. Like most sheep hunters of that day, his northern sheep were the most difficult to get to and came last.

In my time the bighorn became the most difficult of our wild sheep to obtain. It still is, although I'd rate it almost a tossup as to whether the Rocky Mountain or desert varieties are more difficult. Desert permits are more difficult to obtain, but on average the hunting is more successful given a permit. Technically there are six bighorn subspecies today: the Rocky Mountain, the California bighorn, and four desert subspecies. The California subspecies actually grow smaller horns than the largest desert variety, but my purpose isn't to split taxonomic hairs. These days all of our bighorn permits are hard to get, all are worth having, and any tag you can get for any ram offers a great experience!

Never again will sheep hunting be as simple as picking up the phone, but things are starting to look up. Beginning around the 1950s the introduction and reintroduction programs began, and very slowly sheep started to reappear in their former ranges. This job will almost certainly never be finished. There remains vast habitat throughout the West — habitat that used to support wild sheep, or that certainly could.

The progress, however, has been astounding. Although permit numbers are limited, there are sheep and sheep hunting in every state west of the Great Plains today with even a few tags in the Dakotas. After a century of total protection (and continued decline), I never thought I'd see a sheep season in California, but there is one. There are sheep seasons literally within sight of Denver. And, for that matter, Tucson and Albuquerque.

North of the border outfitters in both Alberta and the Rocky Mountain bighorn zones of southeastern B.C. are on a very tight quota, with outfitters receiving from one to four permits annually. Outfitters with track records charge accordingly, as is their right, and permits tend to be spoken for years in advance. Farther west, some of the California bighorn country in the Chilcotin-Cariboo region is not on quota yet. It's a bit like Montana's Unlimited hunting in that it's tough and success is uncertain, but there are plenty of sheep, and hunts can generally be booked a year or less ahead.

South of the border the sheep hunting has been on-again, off-again, with Northern Baja currently closed, and permits available in Sonora and Southern Baja. The permits have been privatized and the hunts are frightfully expensive, but they're doing a very good job of managing their sheep. Success is high, and while neither Sonora nor Southern Baja produce the biggest trophies (historically Northern Baja has produced the biggest desert sheep), most hunters go home with very fine mature rams.

In the United States virtually all the sheep tags are very difficult to draw. Most difficult is probably Arizona, followed by Nevada and the better areas in Montana. I drew one of these, so it can happen, but it takes patience and persistence. If you don't apply, you surely won't draw. Wyoming has lots of applicants, but also gives out quite a lot of permits. Most states now have some system of bonus points or preference points. Odds are so tough in both Arizona and Nevada that, statistically, it isn't ever gonna be easy, but every little bit helps. I was in on the ground floor when Wyoming instituted her preference point system, which is largely why I drew. This is an important point. As the tags become statistically discouraging to draw, the preference point systems will change, and you have to be there when it happens.

Bighorn management is difficult and has not been without its problems. The chief problem is generally disease, and it can be devastating. Some years ago disease swept the Kootenay bighorns in B.C. — and they're just now recovering. Disease ruined some of New Mexico's reintroduced herds just when they were going good. It struck in Texas even before their desert bighorn program had taken off. Arizona's famed Aravaipa Canyon herd had a problem a few years ago and is still rebuilding. The very herd I hunted in Montana developed lungworm that winter and crashed badly.

Right now sheep management is almost a victim of its own success. Numerous transplanted herds, put into ideal habitat with the genetic vigor of expanding into new range, have done fabulously. Reproduction has often been so rapid that within a very years that herd, too, has a surplus available for live-trapping and restocking elsewhere. However, relocation isn't always that simple. There is often resistance to relocation, usually from stockmen's groups — and indeed there's little sense putting sheep in places where they even might be exposed to the domestic diseases they're so susceptible to.

Montana did a great job for so long, and picked some of the relocation sites so well that the sheep not only bred like rabbits, but grew horns like Chernobyl sheep. But right now Montana's relocation program is on hold due to lack of politically available sites (certainly not for lack of suitable habitat). With plenty of money in the bank from auctioned tags, Montana has had to resort to ewe hunts instead!

So, with regrets, I seriously doubt that bighorn hunting will ever be as available as whitetail hunting. I do expect the numbers of tags to slowly increase across the West, but since I doubt that those who want the tags will decline in numbers, it's gonna stay tough. But we all have choices. We can get in shape and assault Montana's Unlimited Permit areas. Or we can save our pennies and go to Canada or Mexico. Or we can apply for every sheep tag in every state that offers them. If you apply long enough, it will happen.

After waiting 21 years for a permit, I said that my own Montana bighorn hunt was anticlimactic. It was. I had allocated six weeks to sheep hunting, and would have used every day if I'd needed to. However, from the first afternoon, when we glassed a herd of more than 40 rams, I knew that success would be a matter of days, not weeks. If the hunt was a bit of a letdown, the shot was not and neither was the ram that shot was fired at.

We'd seen him three days before, early in the morning just as he and his cronies moved into timber. We saw him again that same night when he sauntered back out of the timber — and then bedded in an open basin until dark, keeping us completely and utterly pinned down at a bit over 400 yards away. I well remembered that unlimited permit ram as I made the decision not to shoot. I could have made the shot. Well, at least 8 or 9 times out of 10. But there was black timber all around, it was nearly dark, I was shooting a .270 at a 300-pound ram at very long range, and I'd waited 21 years for this permit. He and his half-dozen buddies, every one a record-book ram, weren't spooked. We would wait and try again in the morning.

Morning came and those rams were gone — and it was *deja vu*. I kicked myself for not carrying a .300, and kicked myself even harder for not taking a shot I knew I could make. I kicked myself for the next couple of days — until we found them again. They hadn't spooked and they hadn't moved. Well, they'd moved, but just to another patch of timber in a little hidden valley about 1,000 yards away. It was almost dark again when we closed in on them. This time the group was larger, all monsters, and when we had them at 125 yards they were all balled up together in fading light.

I'm pretty cool under fire, but not this time. Twenty-one years of waiting and hoping — and more than a couple of failures — weighed on my shoulders. I was completely unglued, and when the chosen ram stepped clear, the cross hairs of my Dakota wobbled across the entire herd, not just my ram. I never got it under control, not completely, but enough to get the shot off. The herd took off across the darkening hillside, my ram trailing, faltering, lying down. The great head was up for just a moment, then sank into the sagebrush. I shook uncontrollably for a long time.

CHAPTER THREE ▪ BROWN BEAR
Hunting the Great Coastal Bears

THE ALASKA BROWN BEAR IS ONE OF THE WORLD'S GREATEST GAME ANIMALS — AND HUNTING HIM ONE OF THE WORLD'S GREATEST THRILLS.

It's about nine o'clock on a lovely spring evening in Alaska. The sun is just going down and the white-coated coastal mountains are slightly pink now. I'm at the tail end of my fourth — and I hope not my last — hunt for the coastal variety of *Ursus arctos* — what hunters call the Alaska brown bear.

In truth the "brownies" are just well-fed grizzlies, but the protein-rich salmon diet combined with milder, shorter winters along Alaska's southern coast have allowed the development of "super-bears" once thought to be an entirely different species. Today we know that there is just one long-clawed, dish-faced, hump-backed bear, and he ranges (discontinuously today) from the mountains of Spain eastward all across Asia, through Alaska, down through the Rockies, and on east to the barrens of Northwest Territories. But even though biologists have long agreed there's just one *Ursus arctos*, hunters continue to separate the bears of Alaska's southern and southeastern coast and offshore islands from the grizzlies of interior Alaska and Canada.

Well they should, for the Alaska brown bear is a true giant of a bear, arguably the largest predator on Earth. The argument is caused by the polar bear. The hides of the largest bears of both species are comparable in dimensions, and the largest skulls are similar as well. Live weights of wild bears of either species are rarely obtained, but since the polar bear is more streamlined for better swimming ability, I'd bet on the brown bear being the heavier of the two.

Regardless of whether the brown bear is truly the largest or merely a tie with his maritime cousin, he's still an awesome creature and in all ways one of the great game animals of the world.

I'll deal with color first since it's the easiest. Brown bears are not necessarily brown. Period. Grizzly bears aren't necessarily grizzled. Period. Some shade of brown, from clover honey to dark chocolate, is the norm for coastal bears, but they can also be very, very blonde — especially on younger bears — or very, very dark. To my knowledge bears of the *Ursus arctos* species are never truly black like a black bear, but they can be so dark as to appear black in binoculars or spotting scope. They can also have the white-tipped guard hairs, but I find the "grizzled" or "silvertip" appearance more classic to mountain grizzlies. Larger, older bears seem unlikely to be light-colored, but that's also not hard and fast. My hunting partner, Joe Bishop, shot a very big and very blonde male on a hunt we shared a few years ago.

The situation is actually very similar with interior grizzlies, except that the silvertip coloration that gives the grizzly its name is somewhat more prevalent.

Hunters may set out with the thought that a honey-blonde bear would make a lovely rug, but size — and an unrubbed hide of any color — is what most brown bear hunters are looking for. The rub comes not from the hide, if you'll pardon the pun. It comes from determining what's big and what isn't. That's very difficult on the hoof — er, pad — and almost equally when the bear is down.

In terms of trophy judgment, I'll fall back on Jack O'Connor's famous line, "The big ones look big." Big bears have big bodies and seemingly short legs, while young bears are leggy and more slender. Big bears walk with a roll and a swagger, but field judgment is very hard, and in this regard it's probably a good thing that brown bear hunters must be accompanied by a guide. Understanding what actually constitutes a shootable brown bear isn't a great deal easier.

Many years ago, Boone and Crockett determined that skull measurement was the one unrefutable, unalterable means of accepting bears into the records book. I agree with this totally. A big skull, measured by length and width added, totaling into the high 20s or more, is proof positive of a great bear. However, skull dimensions are almost impossible to see on a bear, let alone judge. Hunters speak of hide dimensions — and nothing is so easily stretched, if you'll pardon another pun.

With hides we talk of squared measurements. This means a green skin, laid out flat, no stretching, measured nose to tail, and front paw to front paw, the sum of those measurements divided by two.

The Holy Grail is a bear "squaring" 10 feet. I have seen it written that bears squaring 10 feet by honest measurement don't exist. They do, but they're rare. Bears squaring 11 feet also exist, but they're rarer still. And I suspect bears have been taken that square 12 feet and more. On the other hand, it's awfully easy to stretch any 8 1/2-foot bear and turn him into a 10-footer. Some Alaskan outfitters are famous for a little stretching (at least among their peers), but the most blatant example I know of occurred when Russia opened her coastal bears a few seasons ago.

It seemed that all the bears taken were 10-footers, or so the advertisements said, but somehow almost none of the field trophy photos quite measured up to experienced eyes. Russia's coastal bears are also fish-fed and grow large, but the climate there is more harsh, and even at their largest Russian bears probably don't get quite as big as Alaska's best bears.

Stretching the hides a bit is quite harmless, since only skull measurements count, but the danger is that hunters start to expect 10-foot bears. Or reactionaries, aware of all the stretching, claim there's no such thing. Ten-foot bears do exist, just like seven-foot people, but they're uncommon. In truth, they're just as uncommon in the famed areas of Kodiak Island and the Peninsula as they are in Southeast Alaska. The game department's statistics show the average for both Kodiak Island and the Alaskan Peninsula is about the same at plus or minus 7 1/2 feet.

With a good, unrubbed hide, an honest 7 1/2-foot bear (which can easily be stretched into a nine-footer if you must) should be considered a very acceptable trophy. An eight-footer is a very nice bear, and an honest nine-footer is big. Make no mistake, a nine-foot bear by honest measurement will weigh half a ton. Bigger bears weigh more — perhaps much more.

Back in 1981 I was fortunate to take a very big bear on the Alaskan Peninsula with the late Don Johnson and his son, Warren. By honest measurement, laid out on a gravel bar, it measured 10'8" by 11'2", for a square of 10 feet 11 inches if my math is correct. I have no idea what it weighed, but it was one of the biggest things I've ever seen. I've shot many Cape buffalo, and I know a Cape buffalo bull weighs from 1,500 pounds upwards to, rarely, close to a ton. That bear was as heavy as any Cape buffalo I've personally shot — and I know the skin, less skull, weighed over 150 pounds. My guide, "Slim" Gale, was young and tough. I was much younger and stronger myself. All we could do was 100 steps each, then stop and switch packs.

Skull size is the only irrefutable measurement available, but skull size doesn't always follow body size. A bear as big as that (and as old — it was aged at 27 years) might have had a 30-inch skull, but it didn't. By contrast, bears in the nine-foot class might carry record-book skulls. Sometimes you can see that a bear has a clearly outsized head, and that's a good sign. But unlike horned and antlered game, there is no surefire way to field-judge for "book" or near-book proportions. Better to not worry about it and look instead for a well-furred, fully mature bear.

My buddy Randy Brooks, owner of Barnes Bullets, admits now that he was one of the guys who had a "thing" for a 10-foot bear. He made numerous trips and passed a great many superb trophies — some that he now realizes probably reached his goal. He never got a 10-footer, but the bear he finally shot was in the upper nines and is a fabulous trophy. Now that his four years of waiting have expired, he's going bear hunting again, but he maintains that his "10-foot fever" has left him. He'll look for a very big, very mature, well-furred bear, but he's done counting inches on an animal like that that virtually defies precise judgment.

Back when I lucked onto that monster I thought brown bear hunting was pretty simple, except for the packing job. I just didn't know, or appreciate, how truly lucky I'd been. I know better today. In my hunting career to date I've been successful on two of four brown bear hunts; likewise I've scored on two of four interior grizzly hunts. I can absolutely write the brown bear failures off to my own pickiness, slowness, poor shooting, or all three. But even so, that career average is high for grizzly and low for coast brown bears. Nothing is certain on big bears. Fickle weather, more fickle bears, early winters, late thaws (or the reverse), and plenty of tough country preclude sure things. Even so, a good outfitter should come close to 75 percent or better for coastal brown bears, while 50 percent is a very good average for interior bears due to the bears' more nomadic nature.

TOP: Ankle-fit hip boots are the only sensible footgear for brown bear hunting. The terrain isn't all that soggy in most places, but you're constantly wading through rivers and streams.
BOTTOM: This is a very big bear, taken on the Alaskan Peninsula. Aged at 27 years, this one is a very genuine 10-footer — with no stretching and quite a lot to spare.

Conventional wisdom has it that Kodiak Island and the Alaskan Peninsula are the hotspots, but I no longer believe that to be true. They're good — very good — but not necessarily better than Southeast, Prince William Sound, the ABC Islands, or wherever. Big brown bears exist throughout the range, and big bears are simply where you find them. Some of these areas are more difficult to hunt, but are hunted much more lightly and may actually hold more older and larger bears.

In recent years I hunted moose on the Peninsula and never saw a bear except from the air. Likewise, I hunted Sitka blacktails on Kodiak, and while we saw a couple of bears from the boat, I only saw one on the ground. Mind you, I wasn't hunting bears, but in bear country you're always looking for bears, if only so you can stay away from them!

The bear I saw on Kodiak was a wonderful creature, bucketheaded with wind blowing his long winter fur. He came like a cowboy to the chuckwagon bell when he heard me shoot a buck, but was gentleman enough to sit patiently on a ridge above us while we — very hurriedly — boned the meat and made up our packs. As we moved off he swaggered in for his share.

Kodiak and the Peninsula are very, very good, but their reputations and limited permits or seasons carry a premium price tag. The last couple of springs I've been hunting Southeast Alaska with Jim Keeline's See Alaska outfit. It's a good, honest foot hunt in tough country, but the coastal mountains are beautiful and there are plenty of bears — and big bears. There are also numerous wolves and black bear and, around Yakutat, the long-odds chance for a glacier bear, the rare blue color phase of black bear. I've seen three glacier bears on this hunt, an unheard-of number.

The salted hide of the largest of the three is at Jim's base camp now. That undoubtedly used up my luck for this hunt — and that will be okay because it means I won't have to wait four years to follow those great tracks along the gravel bars and glass the big-headed, hump-backed bears on the hillsides one more time.

Tracks along the river are some of the most visible signs of bears — far more visible than the bears themselves. These tracks were made within in the hour.

CHAPTER FOUR ▪ ELK
The Golden Age of Elk Hunting

THE MAGNIFICENT WAPITI — WITH NUMBERS REACHING ALL-TIME HIGHS THE GOLDEN AGE OF ELK HUNTING IS NOW!

My first elk came on Thanksgiving day in 1972. It was in the Pioneer Mountains of southwest Montana with the late John Ward — always good-humored, good company, and a great elk hunter. We picked up two bull tracks in the bottom and followed them clear to the top of the mountain — only to see two yellow rumps sail over a deadfall just as we reached the top. Those elk were gone, except that John knew a big clearcut covered the far slope. We ran like maniacs up to the top and down through the timber, dodging trees and leaping over obstacles. When we reached the edge of the timber both bulls were about 200 yards out into the clearcut and we shot them there.

John Ward loved hunting elk on those timbered Montana slopes. Over the course of several autumns I learned many things from him — one of which was that his was some of the most difficult hunting I've seen before or since! John's preference was to go into the black timber after them, following tracks if there was snow, still-hunting into the wind if there wasn't. He was a magician at getting into the middle of an elk herd — even without cow-talking, which was an unknown technique at the time. We — especially John — did pretty well with "any elk" tags, common in those days. We did much more poorly trying to sort out bulls!

In those days, in that country, there wasn't much choice but to go into the timber after the elk. There was lots of timber, relatively few openings, and not a whole bunch of elk. However, we hunted late when there was plenty of snow, so we had the advantage of tracks and relatively quiet woods. Still, it was very difficult, and what we mostly saw were fresh beds and deep-cut running tracks! One of the great lessons I still

gotten the drop on a mature bull in heavy timber! It's different when they're bugling. Then you have a chance. Maybe the bull will come to you, but even if he won't his bugle gives you a good idea where he is and the game changes. Too, a rutting elk doesn't have his full concentration on staying alive!

This is partly why there are so few rifle bugle seasons these days: The elk are more vulnerable, so more hunting opportunity can be offered later in the fall after the rut is over. I have been on several bugling elk hunts and the experience is fantastic. There is no better sound in all of nature — and certainly no better opportunity to take a good bull. But since I'm a rifle hunter most of my elk hunting experience has come a bit later in the fall when the rut is pretty much finished. This doesn't always mean the bugling is over.

These days, with the autumns seeming to come later, there is often quite a lot of bugling well into October. At this time of year it's fairly unusual to get a bull to actually come to you. But as long as you understand that you still have a huge advantage, you can stalk the bugling bull as effectively as if you'd glassed him. Over the last ten years I've made three elk hunts in Colorado during the first ten days of October. All three times we had a lot of bugling, and all three times those bugles led me to good bulls! Eventually the bugling is concluded, and then you can still-hunt, glass, or play the waiting game. Which is best depends somewhat on the country, but I much prefer the latter two options!

A few years ago I hunted on Slater Creek Ranch up in northwestern Colorado. It was one of those early October hunts, when the rut was on the wane, but the bulls were still with the cow herds. We left the vehicle in the dark, hiking up through big sagebrush hills that led up to timber. My host, Mike Henrickson, told me that the elk fed out into the open at night, then started working their way back to cover in the early morning. Of course he was right. We blundered into one big herd in the dark and I could just barely make out antlers on the bull as he trotted off behind his cows. After spooking that herd we waited until there was just a bit more light. Then, with several bulls bugling at the edge of the timber, we made for an open meadow above a couple of beaver ponds. Mike said that herds often held up there before moving into the timber — and of course he was right again.

We slipped out onto a brushy little knoll overlooking the meadow. The beaver dams and their ponds were right below us, and on across was an open clearcut that rose gently to meet the timber. The opening was literally full of elk, a sea of yellow and tan. I don't know how many branch-antlered bulls were with the herd, but certainly several. We found a likely bull on the left-hand side and I shot him twice. It wasn't seven a.m. yet, and that was the end of that elk season!

Usually things aren't quite that easy, but you never know what you're getting yourself into with elk. Well, that's not true. You know you're going to see some big, beautiful country. That's part of the charm of elk hunting, for in years gone by, in most of the West, the chances for really seeing and shooting elk were fairly slim. This is not the case today; right now elk herds are exploding in the West. Failing a truly catastrophic winter, we're heading into an era of unprecedented elk hunting opportunity — at least since the West was won.

Before the Civil War the American elk existed in untold millions all across the West from the Great Plains on through the mountains and valleys to the Pacific. By the turn of the century, the few survivors had been pushed into the most remote mountains, and the newly-created Yellowstone National Park held some of the last big herds. Numerous populations were wiped out altogether during the excesses of the last century, including, regrettably, the Merriam's subspecies of the Southwest. California's tule elk were barely saved.

Those surviving Yellowstone elk are the ancestors of the vast majority of elk alive today. Live-trapped Yellowstone elk were reintroduced literally all over the continent — from Pennsylvania to Kentucky to Michigan to Oklahoma to Nebraska, and of course to Arizona and New Mexico — and old Mexico, too. This restocking actually began even before the wanton slaughter ended, but in most areas it took many years for the elk to rebuild. Except in the most remote wilderness areas of western Canada and along the spine of the Rockies, there was very little elk hunting from the 1920s until after World War II. Slowly, though, areas long-closed filled up with elk and hunting seasons were reopened. My uncle, Art Popham, a longtime B&C member, drew an Arizona elk tag in the late '30s when elk hunting was first reopened on the Mogollon Rim. He and his English professor and his wife — Jack and Eleanor O'Connor — applied together, drew together, and took superb elk out of that unhunted herd.

By the 1950s most traditional elk hunting areas had reopened. Herds were stable or increasing slightly, and the elk hunting status quo changed very little up until just a few years ago. Oh, there were some changes. Utah opened elk hunting, and more recently Nevada did as well. After decades of careful nurturing California was able to reopen tule elk hunting on a limited basis. There have been limited elk hunts held in such unlikely places as Kansas, Kentucky, and Nebraska, not to mention Michigan and Oklahoma. The demand for tags grew until license quotas, first-come first-served, were established in some key elk states like Montana and Idaho, while other states— Arizona, Wyoming, now Utah and Colorado—went to drawings for tags. Basically, though, elk hunting has changed relatively little in the last 40 years. Until now.

Right now, thanks to a series of mild winters and reasons most biologists don't quite understand, elk populations are exploding. This is a relative thing; if the herds in Kansas or Nebraska exploded it wouldn't be much of a conflagration. However, the herds in Colorado, western Wyoming, and western Montana have exploded. Jack Atcheson, the Butte, Montana booking agent, is probably the most avid and possibly the most experienced elk hunter in North America. Jack tells me he's seeing more elk than he remembers as a kid — elk literally all over the place in his native Montana and adjacent Idaho. This is not without a price, by the way. Atcheson also reports that he no longer sees mule deer at all.

Colorado used to be the court of last resort for elk hunters. When you missed the Wyoming and Arizona draws, got aced out in Idaho and Montana, and couldn't afford New Mexico's private land tags, you could always buy a Colorado elk tag right over the counter and go elk hunting. However, in Colorado that's all you really expected — to go elk hunting. Sometimes you could see elk, but nobody really got elk, did they?

Look again. Colorado now has well over 200,000 elk, with bull/cow ratios on the rise. A couple more warm falls (which reduce the harvest) coupled with mild winters and 300,000 elk could be possible. Right now Colorado has a young, growing herd with few places holding a lot of big bulls — they will follow, but it takes seven to ten years for a bull elk to grow his best

TOP: Many experienced elk hunters feel late in the season, after the snow flies, is the best time for elk. Movement is more reliable and a tracking snow is a great help — but you still have to go high.
BOTTOM: Much great elk country can be reached by backpack — but make sure you're in shape. Packing out an elk is very serious business especially at high altitude.

antlers. Although in good country in Colorado today you will see plenty of elk and good numbers of branch-antlered bulls. In the fall of 2001 I hunted with Lonnie Vanatta at Cross Mountain Ranch, in the Flatheads west of Steamboat Springs. Over the years I have hunted elk in some very good places, but I have never seen more elk, or more bulls, than I saw in that country! Again, this is not without a price. Mule deer herds have nosedived in many areas, especially in the west where elk densities are highest. Colorado used to have a stable elk herd of 100,000 or less — and back then they had a half-million deer. We can't support over 200,000 elk and a half-million deer, and right now the elk are winning big-time.

Why, after literally decades of stable conditions, is the explosion happening now? I simply don't know, but it appears that we can look forward to quite a few years of really fine elk hunting. However, we do have a real problem with most elk herds on public lands, and that problem is a genuine scarcity of mature bulls. Sometimes of bulls, period. We in the magazines, me included, have talked about monster six-point bulls for so long that elk hunters have come to believe their manhood is in question if they go home with less.

Reality is, there aren't enough six-point bulls to go around. Right now, as elk populations explode and, quite literally, threaten the very existence of our mule deer, we need cow elk hunters and we need "any legal bull" elk hunters. And there's nothing wrong with that. Elk may be plentiful right now, but they're still extremely wary and gifted with supernatural senses. Any elk taken in fair chase — especially on public land — is a fine trophy. Any bull so taken is a great trophy. They're not all going to be six-pointers and we as elk hunters can't afford for them to be.

I've used interchangeably the two most common terms for the American version of *Cervus elaphus*: wapiti and elk. "Wapiti" is probably the most proper name, since it comes down to us from the Indians (Algonquin, I believe). "Elk," though more commonly used, is really a total misnomer since it comes from the Swedish word for the Scandinavian moose, *elg*. To this day, when you speak to a European about "elk" you must be very careful to determine whether you're conversing about moose or wapiti!

By either name, our elk is a very large and very strong deer. As part of the *Cervus elaphus* species, our various races of elk are subspecies of a group that ranges all the way around the world in the northern hemisphere. The red deer of Europe, from the Scottish moors and the Spanish highlands eastward to the Caucasus Mountains, are also *Cervus elaphus.* So are the maral stags of Siberia and Mongolia. These days it's become more fashionable to call the marals "Asian wapiti" — and indeed these animals are indistinguishable from our elk. The red deer are a bit different in that they're smaller, darker in color, and tend to have "crown points," meaning a tight cluster of three or more points at the end of the main beam. Regional differences notwithstanding, all the red deer — maral — wapiti are of the same species. However, the animals seem to grow steadily larger as one moves west to east across Europe and Asia. Our elk almost certainly crossed from Asia across the Bering Strait land bridge, along with much of our present and past wildlife. One could surmise that only the biggest and strongest survived the trek — and our elk have not gotten smaller with the passing eons.

American elk may be the same species as red deer, but by comparison ours are giants. We actually have several subspecies of elk. The largest in body (though not in antler) is the Roosevelt elk of the Pacific Northwest, with bulls often ranging from 800 to 1,000 pounds and more. Our most common elk, the Rocky Mountain subspecies, can get that large; I saw a New Mexico bull peg an accurate scale at 800 pounds — field-dressed. But that's most unusual. Six hundred to 750 pounds is a good average range for mature Rocky Mountain bulls; elk of the Manitoba subspecies are about the same size. Tule elk are much smaller, the dwarfs of the wapiti tribe. Big bulls seem to weigh about 500 to maybe 600 pounds. A couple of years ago, I took a good tule elk just a few miles east of my home in Central California. They may call them dwarf elk, but he was still a very big animal!

It should be noted that these weights are for mature bulls. Cows and spike bulls are at least a third smaller, and younger bulls — the 2-1/2 and 3-1/2-year-old four and five-point bulls that make up most of the bull harvest — are at least 25 percent smaller. Mature bull elk — maybe 7 years old, maybe 15 years old — make up a very small percentage of most herds, and an even tinier percentage of the harvest. However, they need to be discussed because they are almost a different class of animal than the rest of the herd. All elk are strong and tough, but a really large bull elk is, in my opinion, one of the hardiest game animals in the world. Anyone who ever said African game is tougher than North American game simply didn't do much elk hunting!

One of America's most classic campfire arguments seems to revolve around suitable elk rifles. Most will agree that the .30-06 is fine, but the real controversy settles around whether or not the .270 Winchester is suitable. It will do the job, but I think it's marginal. Again, there's a big difference between big bulls and the kind of elk normally harvested. The .270 is unquestionably adequate for "meat" elk, but it becomes more and more marginal as you move up the scale to really big bulls. If you're a .270 fan don't get sensitive. In February 2002, I took a very good New Mexico bull — at fairly long range at that — with a single 150-grain Partition from a .270 Winchester. He went down with a heart shot as fast as I've ever seen a bull go down. So the .270 will surely do the job. Even so, I think there are better tools for elk hunting!

Rifles and cartridges for elk can be argued endlessly, but my personal preference starts with a .30-06 with a good 180-grain bullet. Better is a .300 magnum with 180 or 200-grain bullet; and better still is a .338 Winchester or .340 Weatherby Magnum with 225 or 250-grain bullets. For fairly close-range work the .35 Whelen is a wonderful choice, and the .338-06 (a popular wildcat cartridge) would be equally good. At closer ranges both of these cartridges offer magnum performance with very modest recoil. I've also shot several elk with the .375 H&H, and there's nothing wrong at all with choosing such a cannon. In fact, I've got enough respect for elk that there's plenty of reason to choose such a gun. The only problem with the .375 is that it doesn't shoot all that flat. So I'd rate the .338 Winchester Magnum as the best all-around elk gun, an opinion shared by a whole lot of top elk hunters with far more experience than I'll ever have.

To some extent, though, the ideal elk rifle is determined by the hunting conditions. And unlike much big-game hunting,

TOP: A good tule elk, taken in open sagebrush and juniper country along the central California coast. The tule elk has recovered significantly in the last 25 years, with hunting opportunity now increasing annually. Just recently, the B&C Records Committee created a new category to recognize tule elk for the first time.
BOTTOM: This huge-bodied bull with unusual antlers was taken as a "management bull" on the White Mountain Apache Reservation, possibly one of the best places in North America to hunt elk. This bull is almost certainly an old-timer with regressive antlers.

there are really three very distinct periods of elk hunting. The first is the rut, the bugling season.

The bugling season is far and away the most exciting way to hunt elk. Also one of the most successful. It is not as foolproof as it used to be; elk have gotten call-shy in many hard-hunted ranges, and they've also gotten really quiet in some areas. Like all rutting periods, the timing isn't exactly consistent from year to year, so it's easy to plan perfectly and still miss it. Even so, as I said earlier, the bugling season offers enough of an advantage that there are very, very few seasons left that allow centerfire firearms.

To plan for a bugling hunt you need to think about limited entry areas, permit drawings, guided hunts in Canada — or perhaps an archery or muzzleloader tag. In several good elk states the season structure is so favorable toward archery or blackpowder hunters that serious elk hunters are just plain crazy if they don't get involved. Just hearing a bull bugle — especially at close range — has to be one of the greatest thrills the outdoors has to offer. It's a wonderful sound that speaks of pure wilderness. Most of the really legendary elk hunts on private lands and Indian Reservations are held during September, the height of the bugling season — and they're worth it! A couple of years ago I hunted on the White Mountain Apache Reservation. That isn't a hunt a gunwriter can afford, but I had a management tag, which is affordable. I've never seen so many big bulls, nor so many bulls come to a bugle! The bull I took was a nasty, old, downhill, just plain weird elk with huge spiked paddles at the end of his main beams. My friend Terry Hickson nicknamed him "Old Warclub," and I'll never forget the experience!

The next-best time to hunt elk is probably the late season, after the snow flies. Some experienced hunters actually think the late hunt is the very best of all, since the exact timing of the bugling is so fickle, and especially since rifle hunters are banned from so much of it.

In the late season the rut is long since over. The bulls have recovered from their exertions and are starting to move and feed normally again. With winter coming on the elk are starting to get together in herds of increasing size, and of course they're feeding a lot because of the growing cold. Depending on the area and how late the season runs the elk may be shifting from summer to winter pasture, which usually means they're coming down out of the high country.

However, unless the season is unusually late or the weather unusually bad, don't be fooled. It takes really bad weather and serious snow to move elk, and the larger the bull the harder he is to move. Most hunting seasons are long since closed before elk really start to move into winter pasture, obvious exceptions being limit-draw hunts such as the famous elk migration hunt at Gardiner, Montana.

The real advantage to late season hunting isn't that the elk have come out of the mountains, but simply that there's snow. Tracking snow makes all the difference in the world, especially if the elk are in the timber and you have to dig them out.

The third type of elk hunting is everything else! The bugling season isn't on and it isn't late enough for reliable snow — and that often means things are really, really tough. Sometimes you get lucky; you get a freak snowstorm during that "in-between" period, or a late-bugling elk gives himself away. Generally, though, you have to earn your elk (not that you don't even when conditions are perfect!) You can glass meadows early and late, and, if you must, you can dive into the timber and start digging around. "Cow talk" helps immensely with timber hunting. You may not call in a big bull. In fact, you probably won't, but you can calm cows you may encounter and keep them from blowing out the whole world.

Another relatively new thing that helps all types of elk hunting is simply this: A lot more elk. Elk hunting is far more successful than it used to be because we have more elk. We don't necessarily have lots more big bulls, but we have many, many more elk than I was trying to hunt 30 years ago. Sure, we have more elk hunters, too, and that means the licenses aren't going to get easier to come by. But we're coming into the golden age of elk hunting right now, and you don't want to miss these next few seasons. It's good right now... and at least for the near future, it's going to get even better!

CHAPTER FIVE ▪ MUSKOX
North America's Most Under-rated Game

THE LITTLE ARCTIC BUFFALO ISN'T THE MOST DIFFICULT ANIMAL TO BAG — BUT HE'S UNIQUE AND UNIQUELY BEAUTIFUL, AND THE THE COUNTRY HE LIVES IN PROVIDES ITS OWN CHALLENGES.

Except the few guides and outfitters who pursue them, I seriously doubt that any modern sport hunters are genuine experts on hunting muskoxen. They are interesting and attractive trophies, and since they're a bona fide North American game animal a fair number of sportsmen pursue them. However, I doubt that a great many hunt them more than once, and I doubt that anyone hunts them on a regular basis. I am certainly not an expert on muskoxen, but I have hunted them twice, once in fall and once in spring. I suspect that gives me twice the experience of most people who have hunted this animal. To tell the truth, I'd kinda like to go again — so I guess that makes me a real fan of this strange beast!

The Latin name of *Ovibos moschatus* means "musky sheep-ox," which comes pretty close to describing the creature. Biologically he possesses some characteristics of the sheep clan and some of the wild oxen. Like most folks, I tend to simply call them "muskox" in any number. Technically, however, "muskox" is singular and the proper plural is "muskoxen." In appearance he's actually very similar to our bison, and must be a cousin on some level.

However, there is no real comparison in size between a mature muskox and even a half-grown bison. The extremely long hair — all over — makes it natural to overestimate badly the size of muskoxen. They look as big as buffalo, but it's all fluff. Bulls from harsher environments such as Alaska's Nunivak Island and Canada's offshore islands rarely weigh more than 600 pounds, including all that hair and the wonderful horns. Bulls from the mainland are indeed larger, but 750 pounds live weight would be a very big muskox. In other words, they're actually about the same weight as a bull elk!

That long hair that fools you is one of the neat things about this animal. The outer hair is long and fairly coarse; single strands can be as long as 24 inches. Underneath this is a layer of fine wool, called *qiviut* first by Greenland Eskimos and now by most everyone. This wool obviously protects the animal from its extreme environment, and in years gone by was collected for use in sweaters and such. I have a mounted muskox head, and it's actually one of the most striking game mounts I own. At first glance it's huge, but you can stick your arm into that hair almost to the elbow from any angle. My second muskox, by the way, was done like a closed-mouth bear rug, with the head attached. That's a particularly interesting way to preserve a muskox trophy, but you sure don't want to stumble onto the horns in the middle of the night!

Legend has it that the closest you could ever come to getting hurt by a muskox would be to trip over one in that fashion. This is simply not true. I would not go so far as to classify a muskox as dangerous, but they have the equipment and often the temperament to turn tables on the unwary. Their classic circular formation is a primary defense against wolves, but it's not a static circle. Part of this formation is for individuals to make short charges from the circle, then retreat. Bowhunters, who occasionally approach such a circle within, well, within wolf range, have had to do some fast scrambling!

Bulls often group together in twos and threes and can be quite protective of each other. It was exactly this scenario that the great sheep hunter Otis Chandler ran into a couple of years ago. They had shot one bull, but its buddy wouldn't leave. Chandler took a charge from the second bull and was hammered badly. Getting to help, immobile on a sled with a shattered shoulder, must have been a cold and agonizing ordeal.

That's just to say that, as with any wild animal, you can't take chances. It is not to say that the muskox is akin to the Cape buffalo! He's also very easy to spot. In winter a herd stands out from miles away, like pepper sprinkled onto salt. Even in summer, muskoxen are easy to glass in their wide-open terrain. Now, that glassing can take some time, especially on the Mainland, where they range widely over huge country. Finding a bull can take days, however, most generally a herd is found.

Sunsets on the High Arctic are fabulous — but the nights that follow are long and cold!

Muskox hunting is probably the most universally successful hunt in North America.

When Canada first opened many muskox herds hadn't been hunted for decades. Wolves were their only enemy, and it was common for a herd to circle instantly when hunters approached. Today, with more permits and more pressure, getting a shot is a bit more difficult; a muskox herd is more likely to flee than stand when they become aware of the hunters. This has made bowhunting much more difficult, but approaching within range of a centerfire rifle is still not a huge problem in most cases.

The real challenge with muskox hunting is the country and the weather — and that's part of the charm of this hunt. The first muskox hunt I did was clear back in '81, when Canada's Northwest Territories had just started to issue nonresident permits. That hunt was in November and the cold was absolutely incredible.

The hunting day was short, too. As I recall we had sort of half-light from nine in the morning 'til noon, then perhaps two or three hours of genuine daylight, then half-light again from before three until full dark before five. It was just as well; I honestly couldn't have withstood the cold for a longer hunting day!

The second hunt was in the spring, in April before breakup. The days were quite long, and on a couple of clear days the weather was absolutely glorious — perhaps as high as 15 degrees, with a pale sun and little wind. However, we caught a storm on that trip, a serious one. We had the equipment for it; our tent camp could have withstood the gales just fine. But we were luckier than that. We saw it coming as we headed along the coastline out of Coppermine, headed to a crossing across the pack ice to Victoria Island. We made for a little cluster of summer fishing shacks our Inuit guides knew of, and weathered the storm quite snugly.

We had quite a crew on that hunt — myself, Canadian photographer Sherman Hines, gunmaker Col. Art Alphin of the A-Square company, and Col. Charles Askins, last of the old-time gunwriters. Askins entertained through two days of storm with

TOP: Me and Colonel Charles Askins at camp. At 80, Askins was a bit older than your average muskox hunter, but he survived the cold in fine shape!
BOTTOM: I took this fine bull on Victoria Island with the help of my Inuit guide. This was a springtime hunt with relatively mild temperatures, and the very best modern clothing was adequate. In genuine cold, nothing works like the Inuit's caribou-skin clothing!

tales of the old Border Patrol and such, and I only wish I'd had a tape recorder! When it cleared we proceeded across the Queen Maude Strait, set up a very comfortable tent camp, and proceeded to take our muskoxen!

The history of muskox hunting is very old and very new — with darn little in between. At one time the animals were probably incredibly plentiful both in Greenland and the Canadian Arctic, but during the latter years of the last century and the early years of this one muskoxen were badly depleted by trappers, whalers, natives with their newly-acquired firearms, and market hunters. Perhaps surprisingly, some of the worst slaughter occurred right after the great bison herds were finished! Muskox were probably never close to extinction, but there was very little sport hunting between about World War I and the opening of Nunivak Island's transplanted herd about 35 years ago.

A cruise through the muskox listing in **Records of North American Big Game** is fascinating stuff. Even today you'll find a few entries of trophies taken as much as a century ago, and until the minimums were recently raised there were two trophies taken by Admiral Peary, one in 1906 and one in 1909. There are also several entries taken in Greenland in the 1930s. And then you won't find anything until you get to Bert Klineburger's 1959 Nunivak Island trophy.

There have been quite a few transplants of muskox, to places as far-flung as Norway and Siberia, but the Nunivak herd is the best-known and most successful. In 1935 and 1936, 31 muskoxen from Greenland were released on Nunivak. They thrived, with the herd once reaching a high of 750, but generally stable at about 600. On a limited permit basis this was muskox hunting for quite some years, but in 1980 Canada's Northwest Territories began issuing permits.

There was good reason for opening the hunting, justification that remains valid today. After decades of protection, and with little fanfare, Canada's muskoxen herds have literally exploded. From scattered remnants throughout the Far North the herds reached 25,000 in the late '70s, then 50,000 in the '80s. Today they are plentiful enough that permits aren't a problem. Lack of hunters to purchase those permits is today's muskox management dilemma!

For the first few years of Canada's muskox hunting virtually all the hunting was done on Victoria, Banks, and a couple of other offshore islands. The record books began to be rewritten, and that short list of pre-1940 trophies was quickly overpowered by entries from the 1980s. More recently hunts were authorized on the mainland. By 1983 it was obvious that Canada's islands produced bigger muskox, at least in the horns, than Nunivak. By the 1990s it was equally obvious that the Canadian mainland produced the biggest muskox of all.

The real shocker is that with muskoxen, the entire Top Ten were taken or found within the last 15 years. This is unprecedented turnover that is found in no other category. The oldest Top Ten head is from Perry River, Nunavut, taken in 1995. The second oldest are two bulls taken in 1996 near Kugluktuk. Of the other seven, one was taken in 1997; one in '99; the remaining five are from 2000 to 2003.

In years gone by hunters often differentiated between Greenland muskox and barren ground muskox. This was probably a ridiculous and futile effort, since the separation occurred when there was literally no muskox hunting anyway! However, biologists do recognize at least two subspecies of muskox: *Ovibos moschatus moschatus*, the barren ground muskox of the mainland and southern Victoria Island; and *O. m. wardi*, the Greenland muskox of the High Arctic islands and Greenland. On many individuals the Greenland muskox can be differentiated by a white face, while faces are generally dark on barren ground muskox. A more clear difference, however, is almost certainly body size, which is reflected ultimately in potential horn growth. Earlier biologists also identified a third subspecies, *O. m. niphoecus*, the Hudson Bay muskox supposedly found northwest of Hudson Bay and on the Melville and Boothia peninsulas. This subspecies is generally discounted today.

However, it is generally agreed that there are two subspecies, at least in a pure world. The problem is that numerous transplants, plus a broad intergrade area on Victoria Island, have muddied the waters so badly that today most record-keeping organizations just have one muskox category. Probably as it should be. But they just get bigger and bigger — and as the populations continue to grow, probably will for some time.

The traditional minimum score for many years has been 90. When there was almost no muskox hunting — and almost no muskox — that was a formidable goal. On Nunivak it wasn't all that hard to hit 90. When Victoria Island first opened, and today with the mainland being hunted, reaching 90 isn't much of a trick. In fact, the majority of muskoxen taken in the Northwest Territories probably reached the Boone and Crockett minimum had they been officially measured. For those who wanted their name in the book, a muskox hunt was a sure ticket.

In the future it won't be so easy. Since 1992 the minimum score for inclusion in the All-time book has been 105, possibly the largest minimum increase in B&C's history. That, friends, won't be all that easy a mark to hit — and that's as it should be! I suspect there are plenty of muskox out there scoring well over 105. Some herds have yet to be hunted at all, and I suspect we don't yet know how big muskoxen can get. However, it won't be a sure-thing record book hunt with the new minimum, and there are several good reasons.

First, muskoxen are very hard to judge. It's easy to see the drop of the horn and the length of the turned-up tips, but the boss is very important in total score and the full extent of the boss is hidden by that long hair. Since few hunters hunt muskoxen more than once, trophy judgment rests with the guides. With increasing experience many of the Inuit hunters are getting better, but few are really adept at judging, and perhaps it's asking too much.

When I took my first muskox in 1981 I darned near passed it. It looked good to me, but nobody could tell me whether it was a great one or just a normal mature bull. Finally, realizing I might not shoot, my guide suggested a storm might come. So I shot. That bull was the World's Record for several years by another scoring system. In 1993, after it had dried for a decade, I finally had it scored for B&C, and it was 110 and something. But I sure didn't know that when I pulled the trigger.

The other problem is that muskox hunts are generally scheduled to be fairly short — rarely more than a week. Given the bad weather that's likely, hunters generally have the opportunity to see, judge, and pass just a few muskoxen in the course of a normal hunt. And, quite honestly, due to the extreme cold and arduous nature of travel by sled (whether pulled by dog or snow machine doesn't matter — the teeth-jarring bouncing is the same!) few hunters are going to pass a whole bunch of bulls looking for a monster!

I'd personally like to see muskox hunting become a lot more popular. It must necessarily be fully guided, but as ultra-exotic expeditions go, the costs are quite reasonable. As a trophy the muskox is much under-rated. The horns are fascinating, but the long hair and mixture of white, tan, and black are just as beautiful as the horns. However, the hunt itself is much under-rated as well.

In this case it isn't the shot. The shot will probably be quite easy and will probably be anticlimactic, provided you don't get confused by all that hair and shoot low. (In this case, forget the old adage "shoot at hair, not at air." With muskox, the bottom third of what looks like chest is hair. Aim dead center right behind or on the shoulder, not low on the chest!) The stalk will probably be easy, and the glassing easier still.

Ah, but the hunt. Few of us will ever afford a polar bear hunt — and fewer still would really enjoy being out on the ice for two weeks. But a week or so of muskox hunting is a fabulous glimpse of the High Arctic, still North America's least known ecosystem. It's a strangely beautiful place, ferocious when the wind blows and eerily silent when it's still. The Northern Lights alone are worth the trip — and seeing how the Inuit guides deal with their environment is equally worth it.

The Inuits I've hunted with are competent and fearless—and for a hunter from down south, there is much to fear in the High Arctic. Especially the High Arctic itself! But those guys know how to deal with their habitat, and they know how to keep their hunters safe and comfortable. A muskox hunt with them is a short slice of an entirely different existence — and the muskox himself is a wonderful memento of a great hunting experience.

Over the years I have had the good fortune to know some of the truly great Coues' deer hunters. I wish I'd had the chance to talk to O'Connor about them, but I didn't. I did, however, spend a good deal of time with the late George Parker, one of America's greatest hunters — who should be better known than he is.

Parker was the real McCoy — a decorated hero of World War II, rancher, border patrolman, prolific hunter. He put more Coues' deer in all the record books than any other hunter, but he also hunted the world. He was one of very few to take a giant sable in Angola. He collected the Big Five in East Africa, and he hunted extensively in Southeast Asia. His lifelong friend, Colonel Charles Askins, referred to him as "the tough one." Tough, yes, but always the perfect gentleman. And always on the lookout for big Coues' deer bucks.

In Jack O'Connor and George Parker's era Coues' deer hunting was pretty simple. Parker told me they didn't even use binoculars much until well after World War II. Mostly they'd just ride saddle horses through good country, and when they jumped a buck that looked good they'd "bail and blaze." There wasn't much hunting pressure then, and there were lots of deer — especially on the Mexican side of the border where most of O'Connor's hunting was done and where most of Parker's big bucks came from. Those were different times, too. O'Connor himself wrote that they interpreted Sonora's game laws as allowing two or three deer per trip.

O'Connor eventually moved up to Idaho, and as far as I know that ended his Coues' deer hunting. Parker continued to hunt them until he died. Bill Quimby, longtime Editor of *Safari* magazine, hunted with him several times down in Arizona's Canelo Hills. In later years Parker traded his horse for an open Jeep, but the methodology remained much the same — cruise the open, grassy hills characteristic of that area until deer were spotted or jumped. It doesn't sound real serious compared to the way dedicated trophy hunters pursue them today, but Parker knew where to look for the good ones and also knew what a big Coues' deer looked like. His record in **Records of North American Big Game** speaks for itself!

O'Connor/Parker-style Coues' deer hunting can still be done. These little desert deer are thinly distributed over vast country. As O'Connor said, "Even where there are lots of 'em there aren't very many of 'em." However, hunting pressure is also well-distributed and quite light, especially compared to most eastern whitetail range. Buck/doe ratios are fairly high, and although Coues' deer are never easy to find, once located they're actually fairly unsophisticated — again, compared to other "hunter-educated" whitetails. If you cover enough ground, chances are you'll see some bucks.

In January of 2002, I took a very nice Coues' whitetail "the old-fashioned way." I was technically on a desert mule deer hunt with Ernesto Zaragoza, but I got my mule deer early in the hunt, so my Mexican guide and I headed up into the rocky hills — the same hills O'Connor, Parker, and my uncle hunted for Coues' deer and desert sheep — to look for whitetails.

We didn't have the big binoculars or spotting scopes that have been part and parcel to most of my Coues' deer hunting for many years, but we found deer. A doe started up out of a canyon and what looked like a very good buck followed her. We were about 400 yards away and they were moving; I didn't get a very good look, let alone a shot. They topped out and dropped into a little saddle, and we were pretty sure they stayed there. So we climbed the next ridge and approached that saddle carefully.

Perhaps not carefully enough. We were about 150 yards away and could see most — but not all — of the dead ground in the saddle when the doe scampered up the far slope, tail held high. I was certain the buck would follow, so I looked around for something to rest on. There was nothing but waist-high grass and tall ocotillo cactus, so I did the only thing I could do: I wrapped into a hasty sling, got as steady as I could, and waited.

In seconds the buck followed, trotting up after the doe. The view I got was exactly the same, from the rear. The buck was wide, heavy, had good eyeguards, and the back points were good as well. I took the rest on faith. As he topped out he turned to the right, giving me a broadside shot just as he was going into a thick cholla patch. The rifle went off and the deer went down.

He was a very nice old buck, heavy-horned and downhill, but his front points didn't match the rear, so, in terms of score,

TOP: Nearly 20 years have passed since I took my first Coues' deer buck — and I'm still enthralled by these pretty deer.
BOTTOM: Duane Adams spots while I get ready to shoot an Arizonan Coues' buck. These spooky little deer live in great big country, and offer some of the most difficult shooting in all North American hunting.

he wasn't the buck I'd thought he might be. He wasn't a mistake; any old buck like this is a fine trophy. However, this illustrates the two problems with the old-fashioned style of Coues' deer hunting. First, the shooting is generally real difficult. It's difficult enough with Coues' deer; the country is huge and the deer are small, but a bobbing, weaving Coues' buck is a tough target. Add in my offhand shooting position, and it was a hell of a shot, one that I certainly couldn't do all the time. More importantly, however, is that I hadn't properly judged the quality of the deer, so I shot out of a general impression of size rather than actual knowledge. I might have been pleasantly surprised, but I wasn't — and you usually aren't. Over the years I have come to believe that careful glassing with good optics is far and away the best way to hunt these little deer!

My own introduction to Coues' deer hunting was with Warner Glenn and his dad, the late Marvin Glenn, of Douglas, Arizona. Warner hunts pretty much the same way he did back then, with riding mules. It isn't pure O'Connor-style jump-shooting, but a mixture of glassing, covering country, and even some mounted drives. To this day the Glenns' guided hunts are pretty much 100 percent successful, so I don't conclude that Coues' deer have gotten more difficult over the past 20 years. Possibly they've gotten more plentiful now that we're several deer generations into 100-percent limited permit situations in Arizona.

The first time I saw "postgraduate glassing" was with Duwane Adams, a highly successful Coues' deer outfitter out of San Manuel, Arizona. This was a long time ago. Duwane wasn't an outfitter back then, just a Coues' deer nut who knew how to find them. He had 15x60 Zeiss binoculars, an almost unknown product 15 years ago, and he set them up on a sturdy camera tripod and dismantled the hillsides piece by piece. Using this technique, Duwane glassed up one of the biggest Coues' deer bucks I've ever taken, but he'd made me a believer long before we ever found that deer.

Regardless of where you hunt them — Arizona, old Mexico, southwestern New Mexico — I am convinced that pure, serious,

TOP: While Arizona may produce the very best Coues' bucks, the average trophy size is better in Sonora. This is my best-scoring Coues' buck, a nearly perfect 10-pointer, taken with outfitter Kirk Kelso in December 2000.
BOTTOM: Coues' deer country in Chihuahua. There's wonderful country in Mexico's interior; that's the El Nido range in the background, last known stronghold of the Mexican grizzly bear.

concentrated glassing is the best way to get a big Coues' deer today. O'Connor and Parker never hunted this way, but this is the method used by the modern-day Coues' deer gurus. I always thought I knew how to glass, but not like this.

I don't know who came up with the idea of putting ultra-powerful binoculars on a tripod, but Duwane Adams should get a lot of the credit for popularizing the technique. It's ideal for Coues' whitetails, where you're looking for small deer in big country, but it works equally well for virtually any game in big country. Jay Gates, of Kingman, Arizona, probably America's top "all-around deer hunter," uses this technique exclusively today — and he's taken several real bomber Coues' deer. This is the same hunting method used by outfitter Kirk Kelso and his guides. Kelso hunts mostly in Sonora, where there are lots of Coues' deer. On average, hunting down there is more success-ful than north of the border. I believe this is because, on well-managed private lands, the deer are more concentrated, more accessible, and are subjected to less hunting pressure. A num-ber of outfitters, both Mexicans and Americans operating with Mexican partners, are wonderfully successful at hunting Coues' whitetails, but, uniquely, Kirk Kelso does an incredible job at producing big Coues' bucks for his clients.

In Mexico, Coues' deer are plentiful enough that you can hike or ride through the hills — or even cruise ranch roads — and find deer. Kelso, however, hunts them "Arizona style." He uses powerful tripod-mounted binoculars, and he glasses end-lessly from vantage points until a suitable buck is located. Then he plans a stalk.

Although I've known Kirk for years, the first time I hunted in his Sonora camp was in 1999. Coues' deer movement is funny. The weather is generally cool or cold in the morning with sunny middays, and usually one day doesn't seem much different from another to we humans, but there must be differences to the deer. One day you'll see bucks all over the place, and on anoth-er day that seems exactly the same you'll see very few deer. My first hunting day in '99 was one of those days when very few deer were seen. With this in mind, I guess I messed up on the sec-ond day. We glassed several bucks right away, and I probably should have understood that this was a different day. But it didn't click. There was a very nice buck way up on a ridge, and

I took this last-day Chihuahua Coues' deer in a blinding snow storm — not your typical Coues' deer hunting weather. I'm pictured here with Ernesto Beall.

I didn't hesitate. We made a stalk, got in a good position at about 300 yards, and I shot him. He was a nice, clean eight-pointer green-scoring right at 100 inches, a very nice Coues' buck. Except, as the week went on, he eventually became the second-smallest buck in camp!

The next year, the winter of 2000-2001, was an exceptionally good year for antler growth. I went back, and took the best typical Coues' buck I have ever taken, a beautiful heavy-antlered five-by-five (a typical 10-pointer by eastern count). In that particular year this was not only not the largest buck taken by Kelso's clients, but just 1 of fully 14 bucks that topped Boone and Crockett's minimum score of 110 points for inclusion in the All-time records! It take a good year for antler growth to produce that kind of success, but it also takes optics and technique. Kelso uses big 15X and 20X binoculars from Zeiss and Swarovski, tripod-mounted and backed up with a big spotting scope — and he tries not to move on a deer until he's absolutely certain what he's looking at.

There are just four places, at least in terms of political boundaries, to hunt Coues' whitetails: southern Arizona, southwestern New Mexico, Sonora, and Chihuahua. Coues' deer are discontinuous within this vast area, but they're found in most mountain ranges and hills generally between about 4,000 and 8,000 feet in elevation. Far and away the least hunted and least known of these areas is the Mexican state of Chihuahua. I've been down there twice and have taken two nice bucks, neither monsters, but Chihuahua has yielded some dandies. After several years of studying it my overall impression is that Sonora has more deer, so overall success is higher. However, in Chihuahua there are very few outfitters and thus has been very little trophy hunting, so there are some great bucks.

Wherever you hunt them one of the things you can generally expect is beautiful weather in absolutely gorgeous country. The desert mountains are spectacular and — so long as you don't get too close — the dozens of varieties of cacti are dramatically beautiful. But don't bet the farm on good weather! The first time I hunted with Duwane Adams, in Arizona's Catalina Mountains north of Tucson, we ended the hunt huddled under an oak tree in cold rain and fog! The first time I hunted in Chihuahua we were in high country west of the rugged El Nido range, still locally believed to be the last stronghold of the Mexican grizzly. We had several days of high winds with little deer movement — and then it snowed like crazy! On the last day we woke up to nearly a foot of the soft white stuff!

This is always rare, but it can happen almost anywhere in Coues' deer country. Our outfitter, Ernesto Beall, took us into some new country a bit farther south, and when we separated and headed up ridges in the dark the stars were out, but not for long. Shortly after dawn a fresh system came in and visibility was obscured by thick, wet flakes. My guide, Anselmo, and I worked along the edge of a rimrocked butte, glassing down into timbered pockets far below. That's where the deer were, and with the weather getting worse all the time I shot a very nice eight-pointer — and was glad to have him!

There was a time when I hunted Jack O'Connor's deer almost every year, and I still would if I could. These days, quite honestly, Coues' deer have gotten so popular, and there are so many doggone writers hunting them and writing about them that I can no longer place stories about them as easily as I once could. So these days I lay off for a year now and again, and when I do I always miss the desert mountains. Sonora is definitely my favorite place, but I'd like to hunt in Chihuahua again, and it's been too long since I've hunted them in Arizona. The wonderful thing about Coues' deer is there really aren't any bad places to hunt them. The traditional ranges in Arizona produce well, as does Sonora. Chihuahua is very good, and New Mexico's herd seems to be growing and expanding. I haven't hunted them there yet, so I'll have to do that one of these days!

I can't say that Coues' deer hunting is my absolute favorite; I'm very much a generalist and I enjoy — almost equally — a wide variety of hunting. But I can certainly understand why folks get so hooked on Coues' whitetails. They are a uniquely beautiful little deer, and their desert mountains are (usually!) a wonderful place to be in the fall and winter. It might have been a mistake to classify Coues' whitetails separately from all the other "Virginia deer" — but I hope it's a mistake we never correct!

Rocky Mountain (or California) bighorns, they are kept distinct by broad separation between their ranges.

The desert sheep is, of course, just a desert adaptation of *Ovis canadensis*. On the surface he is just a scrawny, tough little sheep, able to live much of his life without water and eke out a living in sun-baked rocks where rattlesnakes and gila monsters have a tough time. His high value to hunters is based, I think, on three things. First, he was made legendary by early sheep hunters like Jack O'Connor. Second is his relative scarcity and the difficulty in obtaining a permit (if not the difficulty of the actual hunting). Third, although his body size is often less than half that of a Rocky Mountain bighorn — a big ram will rarely weigh as much as 150 pounds — his horns aren't that much smaller. Boone and Crockett's minimum for inclusion in the All-time records book is 180 points for Rocky Mountain bighorn and 168 points for desert sheep — less than 10 percent difference in horn size against at least 40 percent difference in body size! At the uppermost end, even a smaller margin separates the World's Records of the two varieties. A good desert ram is spectacular, with horns all out of proportion to his small body size.

Although we typically speak of "desert sheep," in actuality there are four fairly distinct subspecies that we lump together. Northernmost is Nelson's bighorn, *O. c. nelsoni*, generally the sheep of Nevada and northern Arizona. At their most typical these bighorns tend to have flared horn tips with little brooming. In southern Arizona and down into Sonora you find *O. c. mexicana*. For those of us who grew up in the shadow of Jack O'Connor this is the most typical of the desert sheep, small in the body with tight, heavily broomed horns. The largest subspecies, at least based on horn size, is probably the sheep of northern Baja California, *O. c. cremnobates*. After Baja closed there was a lot of poaching in the northern Baja — and in this harsh range there probably weren't many sheep to begin with — but many of the largest-horned specimens have been of this race of bighorn. As you progress down the Baja the sheep get smaller in both body and horn, with *O. c. weemsi* of southern Baja generally the smallest-horned of the desert sheep.

The problem with all this is that nutrition makes a huge difference, so it isn't necessarily accurate to categorize horn size by race. Typically the desert bighorns of mainland Sonora grow tight horns, with rams exceeding about 170 B&C points very rare. Mainland sheep were introduced on Tiburon Island, just a few miles out into the Sea of Cortez. In this "new" range the same darned sheep grow spectacular horns. Similarly, my friend Adrian Sada, a great hunter and Weatherby Award winner, purchased Isle del Carmen off the eastern coast of Baja and introduced *weemsi* sheep into this ideal, but previously unoccupied habitat. In most areas you are hard-pressed to find a *weemsi* that will exceed the low 150s in horn dimensions, but a ram from the original release onto Isle del Carmen appears, at least in photos, as if he will exceed 190 points. So go figure. And don't worry about it. The primary problem with desert bighorn lies in obtaining a permit. Some fortunate hunters can afford to be picky, but for most of us any desert bighorn permit is a wonderful permit — and any place we are allowed to hunt them is a wonderful, wonderful place.

So, in late February 2003, I went to my wonderful, wonderful place, where I had a wonderful permit, hoping to find a good ram. No. That's not true. I would have liked to have found a good ram, and was willing to look for one, but I would have been very happy with any legal ram. While I haven't been lucky enough to draw a tag, over the years several of my friends have. I've tried to learn from them. My publisher, Ludo Wurfbain, drew an Arizona tag a few years ago. He took a nice, mature ram that falls short of huge, and I've heard him describe it in slightly apologetic terms. That drives me crazy. He hunted hard for a long time and took the best ram he could find. By definition it's a great trophy. Tom Gresham, who I co-host the Guns & Ammo Television show with, drew an Arizona tag as a resident. He took the only mature ram he saw. By Boone and Crockett score it isn't large, but it's a very large trophy in his life as a hunter. I was prepared to look for a good ram, but I wasn't going to carry a tape measure and wouldn't be counting up the inches!

Desert sheep mountains rise from the Sonora desert as discontinuous spiky ridges. There are few "big mountains," but many clusters of small mountains. Bighorns were never creatures of the highest peaks, but rather of middle elevations, foothills, and badlands. Similarly, desert sheep do not fear the desert floor. Naturally they will wander across the desert from

TOP: Sheep hunting gear is relatively simple: An accurate, flat-shooting rifle, good optics, and comfortable boots.
BOTTOM: Desert sheep hunting mountains are typically not high, but they're rough, rocky, and surprisingly brushy. I found desert sheep to be one of the most difficult animals to spot that I've ever hunted.

one distant hill mass to another, seeking refuge up in the rocks, but following the rains that bring up new green. If you draw a permit in the States you are generally authorized to hunt your sheep in at least the major portion of a specific mountain range, allowing you to go where the sheep are.

Sonora is a bit different. The permits are allocated to landholders and must be used within the confines of the ranch for which the permit is issued. Some areas, such as the Indian lands, are very large, but some permits are available on relatively small ranches that usually hold sheep... depending on the rains and no recent disturbance.

My permit was for the western slopes and foothills of Pico Johnson, highest peak in the Sierra del Seri range. It is classic and traditional desert sheep country, not far from where Jack O'Connor, Charlie Ren, and my uncle took their "rams from inferno" long before I was born. From the higher slopes you can look off across the foothills to the deep blue Sea of Cortez, and if the angle is right you can see the rugged heights of Tiburon Island. Desert sheep are nomads, following the scant rains, so a big ram seen once may never be seen again — and there is no promise of a given ram being in a given place.

When I flew into Hermosillo, Kirk Kelso was a bit worried. He had taken two nice rams elsewhere, but hadn't hunted this particular ranch. That was good news; the sheep I would be hunting were undisturbed. Kirk and his guides had been doing some scouting, and they'd seen plenty of sheep, which was better news. Not so good was that, so far, they had glassed no big rams. "I don't know, Craig," Kirk said, "we might have to take a ram down in the low 150s. We're just not seeing anything better."

Okay. No way could I afford to do this again, and my permit expired in a scant ten days. I remembered my promise to myself: We'd do the best we could, and that would be good enough. "No problem, Kirk," I told him, and I meant it. "We'll just do the best we can, and I'll shoot whenever you tell me to."

The scarcity and value of a desert sheep permit is such that most modern hunts are quite a production. In the States the fortunate permit holders usually have plenty of offers of help, with people coming out of the woodwork to help glass and share in the fun. Tom Gresham had hunted hard and was at a standstill until some folks left a note in his camp telling him they knew where a decent ram was and if he was stuck he should call them. He got to a phone, made the call, and a day or so later took the ram his newfound friends had spotted. My old friend Ray Salvatori drew one of Colorado's first desert sheep tags. Hunting on his own, he was similarly stuck until the driver of a brown UPS van tracked him down and told him he'd seen a band of rams.

Sonora is more remote, but we had plenty of help. Kirk's wife, Roxann, was along to help glass. Roxie has a superb desert sheep that she took on an Arizona permit a couple of years earlier, and she's a good hand with binoculars. And of course we had Kirk's best Mexican guides, good hands all: Rafael, blessed with the best eyes I have ever seen; the Valencia brothers, Alex and Ramon. Collectively we had a tremendous amount of desert sheep experience in that camp, and all these guys have good optics and know how to use them. I didn't know what we would find, but I was confident we would find the best ram in my area.

As it turned out, "we" was a subjective term. I've got good eyes and have always prided myself on my ability to spot game. In these desert mountains I was totally outclassed! I used to think bighorns were difficult to spot, but they really aren't. Bedded or facing toward you they blend in well, but the prominent white rump patch acts like a beacon that, with good optics, can be seen from miles away. Desert sheep are much more difficult to spot. Small and gray-brown, they are colored just like the jumbled rocks they live among, and are often hidden by the cacti, mesquite, and palo verde that manage to spring from the stones. Their rump patch is smaller and muted, more yellowish than bright white, and while their mountains are not tall they are rough and big. I found these sheep the very devil to spot, and often had trouble seeing them even when I slipped behind a spotting scope or the 20x60 Zeiss binoculars that were already focused on distant sheep.

But we saw sheep readily, plenty of them. Most were ewes and lambs in small groups, but we saw a couple of bands of rams as well. Most were immature, with the largest in a group of seven rams right on Pico Johnson itself. He was not a big ram, but he was mature and legal, and Kirk and his guides had seen him earlier while scouting. Maybe we could do better. So we kept looking, fanning out like the spokes of a wheel, finding vantage points, and glassing into the distance.

There was an old ranch house, long unused, in a little valley below the southwestern tip of Pico Johnson. It was late morning, and Kirk, Roxie, and I were glassing from the yard when one of the cowboys came to fetch us. Ramon Valencia had found rams.

He was set up on a gentle slope at the base of the mountain, glassing southwest onto a series of low ridges. The sheep he had found, two rams, were working their way along a brushy basin well below the skyline. They were in and out of sunlight nearly two miles away. I have no idea how Ramon spotted them, or how he knew that they were worth a closer look. But the feats of vision I have seen these guys perform on Coues' deer are such that you have to take it at face value: If Ramon, Alex, or Rafael say an animal is worth a closer look, you'd better go look.

Through Kirk's tripod-mounted 20x60s we could, with difficulty, make out the two rams. We could see them a bit better through spotting scopes, but the heat waves and mirage precluded accurate judgment. One ram was clearly bigger than his buddy, but the Valencias, using ten-power binoculars, already knew this. Leaving part of our crew to watch them, Kirk and I began to get closer.

The land fell away from Pico Johnson in long fingers, then rose again in a series of ridges, with these sheep on the uppermost ridge. We got a better look at something less than a mile, and Kirk thought we might have something going with the larger of the two. But it was hot now with noon approaching and the mirage was terrible. We would have to get much closer to be sure. So we dropped into the valley and started over the series of ridges. If we were lucky the next-to-last ridge would give us a good look — and if we were even luckier — it just might be close enough to shoot across.

By the time we crept into position on that ridge the rams had bedded on a brushy shelf maybe 80 yards below the skyline. Kirk found the smaller ram readily, but we could only get a partial view of the larger ram. He still wasn't sure, and it didn't much matter — we were still 600 yards out. This ridge dropped into a boulder-strewn drainage, then the main spine rose steeply. It would be ideal to circle the main ridge and come up from behind, above the sheep, but the wind was dead wrong. We looked at it for a long time, and figured just maybe we could go around the eastern end of this ridge, drop into the valley below the sheep, and just maybe get a shot from one of several little rock piles that rose from the valley floor. The sheep would be

My ram is the classic example of the mexicana subspecies, heavy and tight-curled. He was taken with a Remington M700 rebarreled to .300 H&H specifically for this hunt by Rigby's Geoff Miller.

hidden, and we would be hidden from them, but sooner or later they would get up.

Moving slowly and as quietly as we could, we slipped into the valley, at this point probably only 200 yards below the bench where we thought the sheep were bedded. From here the vantage point was terrible, the angle so steep that it was unlikely we would ever see the rams. Trading a bit of distance for visibility, we climbed onto the forward slope of the secondary ridge and set up. We couldn't see either ram, but maybe. We waited perhaps a half-hour, Kirk with his 20x60s on the tripod, me with the rifle over a daypack. I didn't like it — there were several ways the rams could move without giving us a glimpse.

A bit farther down the valley there was a fairly significant pile of boulders jutting up from the valley floor. It would change the angle considerably, so we picked up and moved. I crawled to the forward edge of this rockpile, set my daypack on a likely rock, set the rifle atop it, and snuggled behind it, expecting a long wait.

Kirk set up his tripod just behind me, and he found the ram almost instantly. Far up above us, 330 yards to be exact, was a shelf of black rock. A couple of palo verdes grew on top of it, and the ram was bedded in their shade, just a few feet back from the edge. Just a couple inches lower than Kirk's tripod, looking through the rifle scope with much less magnification, it took me a long time to see him even though I was looking right at him. Finally I realized that the odd circle of light just behind a pale green bough was sunlight off his horns. Then it all came clear — he was bedded, body to the right, and that one horn looked good. In a few minutes he moved his head, and the second horn looked wonderful, too — heavy, carrying the mass well. Now the waiting was much harder!

I don't know how long I lay there behind the rifle. Probably not much more than a half-hour, but the angle was terrible and my neck muscles were on fire — and the pressure was extreme. The shot, if there was one, wouldn't be easy, and it would be one of the most important in my hunting career. If Kirk gave me the word this shot could finish the long quest for a North American grand slam that had begun fully 30 years earlier with a Stone's ram. Of course, this would also be the most expensive shot I had ever made in my life, but I was no longer thinking about that. My "buyer's remorse" was long gone, and I was only thinking about exactly how I would make the shot… and trying very hard not to think about blowing it!

Several eternities passed, and then the ram shifted his head several times. I knew he was going to get up, and he did. He stood broadside for just a moment, the chance I had hoped for, but was still screened by palo verde. And, as good as he seemed to look lying there, we really hadn't yet seen the horns quite well enough. The moment passed, and now he was almost completely screened. Then he turned and walked to the edge of the black shelf and stood on the edge, quartering to me.

He was beautiful, heavy-horned and magnificent, everything a desert sheep should be. Behind me Kirk said, very calmly, "I think you'd better take him."

This I already knew. I figured maybe six or eight inches of wind drift, not quite that much drop; the hold was on his flank, a bit below the backbone. The .300 H&H went off, and the 150-grain Sierra hit him precisely on the point of the on-shoulder, lodging under the skin in the off-hip. Of course I didn't know that. With the crosswind I didn't hear the bullet hit, nor, with the rifle in recoil, did I see it. Kirk, on 20 power, saw the bullet hit, and also saw the second ram, until now unseen, bail off the shelf and scramble up and over the ridge behind. He instantly told me not to shoot again, but I didn't see that ram at all; I had the impression that my ram went off the back of the black rock, then ran hard to the right. And then I lost him in a clump of mesquite.

"He's down," said Kirk Kelso. It was a moment worth waiting 30 years for.

CHAPTER EIGHT - BLACK BEAR
The Elusive Black Bear

ELUSIVE, UNPREDICTABLE, ADAPTABLE, AND AVAILABLE, THE BLACK BEAR IS ONE OF THE UNSUNG HEROES OF AMERICAN BIG GAME HUNTING.

It seems to me there's a relatively small cadre of truly serious black bear hunters, while most North American hunters either take the black bear for granted or ignore him altogether. Make no mistake, the serious bear hunters are indeed serious. Many of them are houndsmen, while many others happen to live in particularly good bear country, but they have in common a fascination for the American bear, old *Ursus americanus.* I can understand this, for there is much to be fascinated about — and much to recommend the hunting of this elusive creature.

One aspect is quite simply his availability. I am personally fascinated by all bears; they're beautiful, exciting — and sometimes frightening — creatures. But due to the scarcity, difficulty of logistics, and just plain cost, few of us will hunt grizzly or Alaska brown bear more than once or twice in our lifetimes, if at all. Ditto and double for polar bears. As crazy as I am about bear hunting, I have long since accepted that I will probably never hunt a great white bear. The black bear is every man's bear.

He actually occupies the widest range of any North American big game animal. You can find him from Florida to Newfoundland and from Mexico to Alaska, and with the exception of the Great Plains you can find him almost anywhere in between. Mind you, the black bear is not as plentiful as our deer, elk, and moose; he requires space and some measure of solitude. Given those, however, he is an amazingly adaptable creature. You'll find him in the swamps of the Deep South, in the desert mountains of Arizona and old Mexico, in the forests of the Upper Midwest, literally throughout the western mountains and on north all the way to treeline.

The black bear is, of course, not huntable throughout his present range. In general, his population is increasing and there is black bear hunting in every region of the United States and all across Canada. At least partly due to this huge distribution and widely differing habitats, bear hunting techniques are surprisingly regional.

Hound hunting is probably the oldest technique, and certainly the one steeped in the most tradition. Daniel Boone was a houndsman; so was Congressman David Crockett of Tennessee. Hound hunting is a technique best-suited to forested mountains — the forest because in unbroken forest the unaided man would almost never see a creature so shy and elusive as the black bear; and the mountains because the ridges and hollows make it possible to follow the hounds' music for great distances, while in level forest bears and dogs will outdistance the hunters all too quickly.

In forested country, and especially in the fairly flat forests of the Great Lakes region and much of central and eastern Canada, the option to hound hunting is baiting. The black bear's eyes probably aren't quite as weak as legend would have it, but he relies primarily on his ears and nose in avoiding danger. These last two senses are keen enough that, in thick country without open vistas, a human has very little chance of encountering a bear on purpose. However, one of any bear's few weaknesses is his greedy stomach. As we shall see, baiting is no more of a sure thing than use of hounds, but it is an effective black bear hunting technique.

The last of the three primary methods is spot-and-stalk hunting. This simply means spotting or glassing up a bear at some distance, then planning an approach. It's an enjoyable and effective technique, but it has one major requirement: country open enough and with enough relief so that bears can be seen.

In addition to these three primary techniques, there are two more worth mentioning: calling and tracking. We will dispense with these two methods right now, then talk about the three primary techniques of hound hunting, baiting, and spot-and-stalk in greater detail.

TOP: I took this nice Manitoba black bear over bait with the help of trapper Don McRae.
BOTTOM: A beautiful cinnamon bear taken on a horseback hunt in southern British Columbia. This is not a big bear, but the lighter color phases are often smaller bears, taken for color and beauty rather than size.

For reasons unknown to me, calling for black bears was pretty much confined to the mountains of southern Arizona for many years. Today, as both hound hunting and baiting are becoming outlawed in more and more regions, I look for calling to become a more popular method. Black bears will respond to a varmint call.

A common dying rabbit call will work, and a fawn bleat is better. Like all calling, it won't work all the time, but it does work based on two primary criteria. First, a bear must hear the call and be fooled by it. Based on scouting, you must choose your calling sites where bears are likely to be; and you must work the wind so that you will see the bear before it smells you. Second, the bear must be in a mood to respond — hungry and not otherwise occupied. This last is beyond your control, but it's a primary reason why no calling of any wildlife is effective all the time.

To call bears, you must choose your ground with care and be persistent; you can expect to call from many more stands per bear than, for instance, for each coyote you might call in. However, you must also choose your calling site with caution in mind. When bears come to a call it's often an aggressive male that responds, and charging the call is not uncommon! It's best to call in pairs, with two hunters watching each other's back.

Tracking is problematic simply because suitable conditions — soft enough ground or snow—are relatively rare. However, should you encounter the fortuitous circumstances of tracking snow or mud, an open bear season, and fresh tracks, it is quite possible to track a bear to a shot. I'm given to understand that some of the huge bears Pennsylvania has produced recently have been tracked in the snow during that state's very short — and fairly late — fall season. Let's turn back now to the three primary black bear hunting methods, starting with hound hunting.

These days it's popular — even among hunters who should know better — to revile the houndsmen and consider pursuit in such fashion as somehow less than fair chase. This irks me immensely. It's no different than the many other controversies among the diverse groups of hunters: bowhunters looking down on gun hunters; traditional archers feeling superior to the compound crowd; buckskinners versus the in-line muzzleloader crowd; even meat hunters versus trophy hunters. We as hunters have enough trouble from the outside without picking each other apart.

Hound hunting is different from most other hunting techniques, but it is neither easy nor simple. The thing about it that must be understood is it's the houndsman who has the primary input. If you or I, who are not houndsmen, go on a hound hunt for bear we can have very little direct input on the conduct of the hunt. The houndsman, however, has trained his hounds from puppies. His primary pleasure is in listening to his hounds and watching them perform. In hound hunting the shot is actually nothing — a simple and quick end to the chase at very short range. The pursuit is everything... and most houndsmen do most of their bear hunting on a pursuit-only basis, with no intention of killing the bear at the end of the chase.

Following the hounds on a pursuit-only basis is about as close to catch-and-release fishing as there is in the hunting world. However, in terms of taking a bear, hound hunting has a couple of unique and attractive aspects. First, it is probably the single most physical — and most physically challenging — way to hunt bears. When you start a hound chase you have absolutely no idea where the chase may lead you, or what might happen. It is hardly a sure thing. The odds are very good that the bear will outdistance the hounds... and even better that the chase will outdistance the human hunter. When that happens you can count on many hours, perhaps days, in recovering the pack before the hunt can continue.

To prevent this it's essential that the human hunters keep up with the chase, which means running, crawling, and scrambling through whatever horrible real estate the bear has led the hounds. Sometimes horses or road networks allow shortcuts. And, admittedly, on average a hunt with a good pack of hounds is probably the most successful of all bear hunting techniques. But only for hunters in good shape who are willing to hunt very hard. It usually isn't easy.

The other unique aspect about hound hunting is that it is far and away the most selective of all bear hunting techniques. I'll admit something right here and now. Despite a lot of experience with black bears, I still have trouble properly judging them. There is never an excuse for a hunter to make a mistake and take a sow with cubs. At the opposite end of the spectrum, a truly huge bear will always look huge, and that's a hard mistake to make. But there's a vast middle ground between smallish bears and mature trophy bears.

feel right at home. There is a parallel with hound hunting in that, as the houndsman himself gets the most satisfaction out of hound hunting, the person who sets the baits and builds the stands gets the most out of bait hunting. It is not as easy as it sounds.

The bait must be set in an area where a bear will find it, and where he can approach in cover thick enough so that he will have the confidence to approach in daylight. Siting of the stand requires sound tactical decisions so that the bear can approach without winding the hunter... and offer a clear shot.

Baiting is the method of choice in the unbroken forests of Canada from central Saskatchewan eastward, and is practiced in Alberta and a few U.S. states as well. Hunting over bait is not quite as controversial as hound hunting, but it too is under fire and has been outlawed in several areas. Those who look askance at baiting need to look at the local conditions before they judge. In Oregon, for instance, both hounds and baiting are now illegal. Oregon has a very high bear population, but in the dense forests of the western part of the state, sans hound and sans bait, there is darn near no other way to hunt bear effectively. Those among us who cast stones at baiting for bears should also keep in mind that more than a dozen U.S. states allow baiting for deer. Local hunting techniques are usually the result of traditions dictated by local conditions, and outsiders shouldn't be quick to judge.

I will admit that I get stir-crazy in any stand, whether I'm waiting for deer, bear, leopard, or whatever. However, sitting over a bear bait is a very exciting experience. When the bear comes he comes silently and suddenly, appearing on the edge of the clearing almost like a ghost. The light is usually poor and the shot must be very sure, for there will almost certainly be near-impenetrable cover just a few steps away. Nobody wants to go into that gloom after a wounded bear!

Baiting is probably the second most selective bear hunting technique. The light may not be good, but the distance is usually short — 50 to 100 yards. Also, in setting up the bait and blind you can establish known size references such as the bait itself or marks on trees just in case a small bear tries to fool you.

Every bait hunter has his favorite "formula" for surefire bear bait. A favorite among trappers is beaver carcasses, while others prefer stale pastries, winter-killed carcasses, fish offal, and a wide variety of other noxious treats. I'm not sure it makes a lot of difference, but the bait must be set so the bear has to come into an opening — as small a clearing as possible, for confidence — and it must be anchored so he cannot drag it away. I've sat in bear stands from Newfoundland to Alberta, and the circumstances are quite similar throughout. The method is very successful, but the degree of success depends largely on the density of the local bear population and how undisturbed they are. On a hunt with Trapper Don McRae in Manitoba, for instance, I saw more than a dozen different bears come to bait in a week's time — and when you're seeing that many bears, bait hunting is wonderfully exciting.

Spot-and-stalk hunting, or glassing, is the purists' method of choice. I suppose they would have us believe that it's the only genuinely fair chase method, and thus is the only method that should be legal. Problem is it simply won't work in all areas. You must have enough openings so that, sooner or later, bears simply have to cross or feed where they can be seen. Then there must be enough relief so you can see those openings. Finally, the bear population must be dense enough and undisturbed enough so that they aren't totally nocturnal and can be seen in daylight. Colorado, for instance, where both hound hunting and baiting are now illegal, easily meets the first two criteria. But lots of people use the Colorado mountains and the bears, though numerous, are quite nocturnal. Except for some wilderness areas, I wouldn't choose that state for spot-and-stalk hunting. Western Oregon has plenty of relief and lots of undisturbed bears—but openings are few and far between.

However, where conditions are right spot-and-stalk hunting is quite practical, and it is indeed one of the most enjoyable ways to hunt black bear. This is the traditional technique in British Columbia, Alberta, Alaska, and Montana... and in areas like these with lots of bears it is particularly successful.

A few years ago I hunted black bears in southeast Alaska, way south out of Wrangell. That part of Alaska holds the heaviest forest I've ever seen, and on the surface glassing for anything would be impossible. However, in the springtime the bears cruise the beaches searching for offal and munching the green grass that sprouts at the high tide mark. It was basically an unguided hunt that Lad Shunneson organized; we were four hunters on a fishing boat, and we could fish for halibut and salmon through the day, then cruise the inlets in small boats in the evening looking for bears. In five days we had four bears on our boat, which is about as good as unguided bear hunting can be.

Over the years I have done more spot-and-stalk bear hunting than by any other technique. This is largely through chance, but also undoubtedly because glassing is my own favorite hunting technique. Probably because I've done more of it the best black bears I've taken have all been spot-and-stalk. Twenty-five years ago I shot a monster in southern B.C., big enough that the taxidermist felt it worthwhile to steal the skull. A few years later some burglars completed the loss by taking the rug along with everything else.

That was my biggest bear, but I've taken a few others that were close. One was a fine bear I shot with outfitter Jim Keeline near Yakutat, Alaska in 1994. That bear was a fairly classic situation in that we glassed him up one day and shot him the next about two miles farther down a big, open face. It was a half-day stalk in very steep, rugged country, truly a great experience. In 2001, after hearing about the great bear hunting there for years, I hunted on Vancouver Island with outfitter Jim Shockey. The island is heavily wooded, with the only real opportunity to glass bears in the clearcuts and on logging roads. Despite this we glassed lots of bears — more than 25 in one day alone! My guide, Guy Shockey, is the only person I've ever hunted with who had enough experience with bears to judge them by skull size. He called mine at "more than 19-1/2 inches, but less than 20." He was right!

One of my best bears was taken with some friends in coastal North Carolina, but I don't know exactly how to describe the technique. It was during the fall season, and we were hunting from deer stands over cornfields. The bears were coming into the corn to feed at night, but when you glassed a bear from an elevated stand it was necessary to stalk him. So I guess this was a combination of baiting and spot-and-stalk!

Spot-and-stalk hunting has its drawbacks. It is absolutely the least selective method because even the most experienced hunters can make mistakes. A case in point was that unguided black bear hunt I made in southeast Alaska. Shunneson and I were hunting with Randy Brooks of Barnes Bullets and Fred Gonzales of Northern Outfitters clothing, a good, experienced crew — except neither Fred nor Randy had ever shot a black bear. Fairly early one afternoon from the big boat, we spotted a bear along the beach by a big log. He had all the marks of a good-sized bear; his head seemed small, his body was round, and he seemed to have a broad behind.

Randy, Fred, and I jumped in a skiff and headed in, with Fred as the designated shooter. The way the wind was blowing we needed to approach from behind the downed log, which permitted only occasional glimpses of pieces of bear as we closed. Finally, at 40 yards, Fred thought he could clear the log enough for a shot. Not quite; he didn't allow for the difference between scope and barrel, and his bullet dug a deep furrow in the log and sailed out into the bay. The bear turned and sauntered into the jungle — and he still looked pretty good. We went back to the big boat for supper, then Lad and Fred went one direction in one skiff while Randy and I went the other.

Later that evening, while cruising the shore, Randy and I spotted the same bear. I know it was the same bear because, later, I checked the tracks. We stalked him from the other direction and Randy flattened him with a lovely shot at about 150 yards. Except it just wasn't a big bear. Reasonable, maybe even respectable, and with a lovely hide, but a long ways from the bear I thought he was. Since I have shot a lot of black bears and Randy has not, it was my fault altogether, but on black bears you must be very careful to avoid "ground shrinkage." Look for small ears spread wide apart and avoid Mickey Mouse ears. Try to look for a ponderous, swinging walk. As Jack O'Connor said, the big ones look big, but with black bears, the small ones sometimes do, too!

I'm not sure there is any real limit to how big black bears get. I have shot three that squared, without stretching, over seven feet. That's rare, but I have seen legitimate eight-foot black bears and heard of at least one nine-footer. This, of course, is well beyond average grizzly size and well into Alaska brown bear size. Such bears are very rare, but they exist. The obvious problem, of course, is that body size doesn't always translate exactly into the skull size, which is all-important for record-book measurements. I do agree with skull measurements, since no measurement can be "stretched" more than the hides of bears and cats, but no one can judge a skull on a live bear except to say "that bear has a big head."

I believe most areas can produce giant black bears, given good feed and the opportunity for bears to fully mature. Surprisingly, Pennsylvania produces shockingly huge bears, despite heavy hunting pressure. Another oddball hotspot is coastal North Carolina, and perhaps even more odd — unless you've been there and seen the country — is California, both the northern and southern mountains. Then there are the more traditional big bear hotspots: central Arizona's mountain ranges, Newfoundland, Vancouver Island, the Queen Charlotte Islands, southeast Alaska. And one shouldn't overlook Manitoba, northern Alberta, and southern British Columbia. In fact, there are just a lot of places that produce good bears!

We all dream of huge bears, but what most of us really want is a well-furred rug. With black bears that can mean a rug in a wide variety of colors, but most of the color phases of black bears are somewhat regional. "Basic black" often includes a white star at the throat, and in many areas black is darn near the only color. This is generally true in the East, likewise in most of southeast Alaska, while throughout much of central and western Canada and the western United States at least some percentage of the black bears are some shade of brown. Occasionally, as is the case in northern California, brown is actually predominant.

A "brown black bear" may run in a variety of shades, from blonde through the gingery "cinnamon bear" to various shades of reddish and chocolate brown. It is my experience that the lighter shades, especially the prized blonde and cinnamon colors, are usually smaller bears. Radiotelemetric research has proven that bears do sometimes change color in their lifetimes — from brown to black, even — and it is likely that very light bears will darken with age. For darn sure, if you take a big blonde or cinnamon bear you have a great prize.

The two most rare color phases of black bear are very localized. The Kermode bear, confined to the Queen Charlotte Islands and protected for many years, is a white black bear. Not an albino, he has black eyes and claws with a very white or yellowish-white coat. My uncle and longtime Boone and Crockett Club member, Art Popham, took one on a museum permit some 40 years ago. It's mounted in the Kansas City Museum of Natural History in a diorama with a black black bear, and is a most dramatic creature.

The other localized color phase is the so-called glacier bear or blue bear. Like the Kermode bear, this is caused by a recessive gene, meaning that where the gene pool exists a black mother can have a blue or white cub; or vice versa. The glacier bear is found basically within 100 miles north or south of Yakutat, Alaska, and is huntable on a black bear tag, but (again quoting O'Connor) even where there are lots of 'em there aren't many of them.

On a second hunt in that area in 1995, again with Jim Keeline and guide Jack Ringus, I actually saw three glacier bears, a massive herd of such things. They vary immensely, as do all color phases. One, a small bear, was very gray with black head and stockings. Another, a big sow with a pure-black cub, had silver streaks all down her side. The bear I shot was a very big, very old boar. Perhaps, as a cub and younger bear, he had looked like that gray bear I saw. As he was, in dim light he looked very black, but in sunlight he turned powder-puff blue. We watched him and stalked him for three days before getting a shot, and when we finally got him I found the blue tint to be caused by an underlayer of very fine, white hair.

With any of the unusual colorations, you really can't hunt for size. If I could have gotten a shot, you bet I would have taken that gray glacier bear I saw. Over the years I've taken two beautiful cinnamon bears, neither large, and I didn't hesitate. Someday perhaps I'll see a blonde black bear, but I never have. On the other hand, if you prefer size over color, you can hunt for that instead.

The wonderful thing about black bears is that there are plenty of them and the hunting is economical. You never need to feel like a black bear that you pass up is the only one you'll ever see. And yet, like all bears, there's that special element of caution when you're hunting them. No, they aren't really dangerous, but they can sure turn the tables if you make a mistake. I don't know anyone who has been mauled by the unquestionably more dangerous grizzly bear, but I know fully three good black bear guides who have been seriously mauled by black bears. No, I don't want to get mauled and I don't want to get charged, but the possibilities make life more interesting.

CHAPTER NINE ▪ MOUNTAIN GOAT
Lord of the Crags

THE SHORT-HORNED, LONG-HAIRED LORD OF THE CRAGS IS ONE OF OUR MOST UNDER-RATED BIG GAME ANIMALS!

This business of writing about hunting and guns isn't all that easy. There are, after all, only so many ways to hunt deer and so many things to be said about the .30-06. Therefore I suppose we writers can be forgiven occasional flights of fancy in developing catchy titles and offbeat slants for what really are "business as usual" stories. I, of course, have been equally guilty.

However, over the years I've seen a number of writers (and/or helpful editors) try to stir up additional interest in a story about hunting the Rocky Mountain goat by calling it "the poor man's sheep hunt."

This offends me. It is true, thank goodness, that hunting our mountain goat on a guided hunt basis is far less expensive than sheep hunting. But does the phrase mean that the mountain goat is worthy of only a working hunter's attention? That there is more worthy quarry for the wealthy? Or does it mean that the mountain goat is some sort of backward cousin to the more noble sheep? These premises and any extensions thereof are simply preposterous and are a great disservice to both a superb game animal and those who might pursue him. Serious goat hunters — and there are a few — got a huge boost in 2001 when two British Columbian hunters were awarded Boone and Crockett's highest award, the Sagamore Hill trophy, for taking the new World's Record Rocky Mountain goat on a difficult and grueling self-guided hunt. This may create a bit more interest in hunting this beautiful animal!

Our unique Rocky Mountain goat is not a cousin to any sheep, backward or otherwise. He is a majestic and challenging trophy in his own right, and I consider it a blessing, not an indictment, that he can be pursued for a fraction of the cost of a sheep hunt. Unfortunately, since both Rocky Mountain goats and our American wild sheep are high country animals, some parallels must be drawn. In this regard, goat hunting is both more difficult and much easier than sheep hunting.

In good country, goats are extremely prolific and can become quite plentiful. They are normally found above timberline and are relatively sedentary in their habits. Their year-round white coats make them extremely prominent in the ledges and crags they prefer. These facts combine to make Rocky Mountain goats relatively easy to locate at long range, certainly easier than any sheep, except Dall's sheep before the snow flies.

It is also much easier to shoot a goat than it is to shoot a sheep — provided your goal is simply to shoot a goat. With goats there are no 3/4-curl or full-curl minimums nor a requirement to count annual rings. Under most circumstances both billies and nannies are legal game. This is probably because the horns of both sexes are quite similar; those of the nannies tend to be long and slender, while a billy's horns are thicker. Both genders, however, carry short black daggers that curve back and slightly out from bases just above the ears. A difference in length of just two inches can separate mediocre from outstanding. Thus, if your desire is to simply shoot a goat, in decent country you can do this in a day or two of hard hunting and be done with goat hunting.

Such was my first experience with the Rocky Mountain goat nearly 30 years ago. The goat was part of a mixed-bag hunt in northern B.C. When it was time to get a goat we simply climbed up and got one. Mind you, it wasn't all that easy. In fact, it was probably the most physically demanding day I'd spent hunting up to that point in my career — and I was young and in great shape, fresh out of Marine Corps officer candidate school.

This was in late August, when the goats' pelage is short, patchy, and ugly. The result of that day was a particularly long-horned nanny goat. Despite the poor hide and the sex of the trophy, that remains a memorable day and its result a prized trophy. However, many years passed before I really understood what goat hunting was all about.

If you want to hunt goats and just perhaps take a fine goat — rather than just shoot a goat — the game changes dramatically. Goat hunting is then no longer just a difficult physical

There's really just one way to get up a goat mountain: on foot. This mountain is much steeper than it looks and it got much worse minutes later.

exercise, but a gruelling mental challenge as well. Here's where goat hunting becomes more difficult than sheep hunting.

While it's often far easier to locate goats, it's usually more difficult to get to them. It's axiomatic but true that goats live in rougher country than sheep. In fact, goats often live quite happily in country so rocky, steep, and treacherous that sheep will not — perhaps cannot — tread. Horses are a limited advantage in most sheep hunting; sooner or later you must leave them and eventually you must come back to them. In goat hunting that "sooner" is often much sooner!

If you can reach them and, preferably, get above them, then goats are usually not all that difficult to approach. Among their high crags they are confident in their security and a close stalk is likely, but that's a big "if."

Goats subsist on much rougher forage than sheep. They don't need the grassy basins and can make do nicely on the sparse, but nutritious, grasses and forbs that grow among the rocks. Especially the older billies that may spend virtually all of their time on narrow benches or ledges, never revealing even a clue as to how they got there or how — if — they ever leave their sanctuary. Two factors must be considered in planning a stalk on a goat. First, how to get there safely. Second, how to recover the goat safely. Sometimes the first condition is impossible to meet; the second often is.

In the summer, when the rocks are dry, goat country is steep and treacherous. Later, when the pelts are most prime, those rocks are frozen and deadly. Common sense and sound judgment must be applied when planning a stalk, and it must be thought through all the way. Sometimes you can approach to shooting range, but if you shoot the goat you can't get to it. And if you can get to it, can you get yourselves and goat back out? Often you have to walk away. Or, rather, you have to climb away, for only rarely are the obstacles so obviously insurmountable that no stalk is attempted.

If it doesn't work one way, perhaps you can try a different approach. Or perhaps you can wait in the hopes the goat will move to a more accessible spot. Sometimes they will, but often you're better off looking for a goat you can reach!

Whichever, only common sense can mitigate the very real dangers of goat hunting. Never go it alone, especially in an unguided situation, and don't let goat fever push you past your mountaineering capabilities. I've been stuck for long, horrifying minutes, unable to go up or down — and I've felt my feet slide on icy rocks with nothingness inches away. I always carry an ice axe on mountain hunts these days, and on late hunts crampons make sense, but it's far better to stay out of situations where you might need either, let alone climbing ropes and pitons.

That's getting to the goat. The next, and possibly larger question, is exactly what kind of goat you're getting to. *Oreamnos americanus*, the Rocky Mountain goat, is a unique genus and species found only in the mountains of western North America, naturally from the northern Rockies and coastal ranges on north to southern Alaska. He has been transplanted, and has done very well, as far south as Colorado and Nevada, equally well on Kodiak Island. The heart of his range and the bulk of his population is found in British Columbia's mountains and adjacent southeast Alaska, but northern B.C. seems the limit of the goat's ability to withstand northern winters. Just a few extend up into the Yukon and the Mackenzie Mountains of Northwest Territories.

The mountain goat is not a true goat of the *Capra* genus, but rather a *rupacaprine*, or goat-antelope, somewhat similar to Old World animals such as the European chamois and the goral and serow of the Himalayas. Note, however, that he occupies his own unique genus with just one species; like the American pronghorn, he has no close relative on this or any other continent.

There is a great disparity in physical size among individual goats, but a large billy can exceed 300 pounds and will seem much larger in his flowing winter coat. The horns are small, which probably accounts for his second-rate status among trophy hunters. A billy with eight-inch horns is minimally acceptable. A nine-inch billy is perfectly shootable. A ten-inch billy is fabulous. And of course the nannies have horns as well, and virtually all goats have horns in relation to body size. These factors combine to make the Rocky Mountain goat the most difficult of all North American animals to judge. I'd be lying if I said I was good at it — and so is anyone who claims to be foolproof at judging goats!

The charm — and heartbreak — of goat hunting is you must get close to be certain. There are, of course, long-range indicators of sex and size. Herds, especially with young ones, are unlikely to have trophy billies among them, but if there is a big billy temporarily in a family herd he will dwarf the rest. In general, though, mature billies are likely to be in twos or threes or solitary, and they're likely to be in higher, rougher, more inaccessible crags than the nanny herds. Typically a billy will have a slightly off-white, yellowish cast to his coat, and the billies will come into long winter coats well ahead of the nannies.

These clues will make you climb a mountain for a closer look, but they aren't definitive. The horns are, of course, but the horns are the very devil to judge. Yes, the billies have heavier bases. But heavier in comparison to what when you're looking at a lone animal of unknown size from several hundred yards away?

When push comes to shove, you must be very close to be certain both of sex and size. The best way to be 100 percent certain is to see the black, pad-like glands at the base of the horns. Both males and females have this gland, supposedly used to mark territories. However, the gland is much more prominent in billies and, at close range, will be visible — whereas, in nannies, the horn glands are concealed by hair. To see this feature you need patience and good optics — and you'd better be close.

With most open-country game, certainly with sheep, you can make a sound shoot/don't shoot decision long before you're in rifle range. On a calm day with a decent spotting scope you might decide that a ram meets your standards from a mile away, but certainly at a half-mile. The selection is made and the stalk is simply closing the deal; when you reach your shooting position, be it 30 or 300 yards, all that remains is a last-minute check to make sure you have the right animal. This is not so with goats. At a distance you will have subtle indicators of size and sex, but it's a mistake to anticipate a shot at the end of a stalk. First you have to get close. Once you've closed in and you can see the black pads at the horn bases, then it's time to get serious about final evaluation of the horns.

How close you must get depends on optics, terrain, weather conditions, and of course how particular you are. A goat hunt is one of the very best places for a variable-power spotting scope with an upper range of 40X or 45X. Twenty power really isn't enough past a couple hundred yards, but in the mountains it's a rare day when it's calm enough to really use extreme magnifi-

TOP: *This northern British Columbia Billy was taken in late August. Billies tend to get their winter coats much earlier than nannies, but the later the better for the very best pelts.*
BOTTOM: *Goat country in southern British Columbia. In country like this, mature billies die of old age without ever seeing a hunter.*

admire a lifesize or half-life mount of a Rocky Mountain goat. I've even seen them done as a stunning rug mount, head attached, but not for the floor. I wouldn't want to trip and fall on those horns!

There is a down side to old *Oreamnos americanus*: his flesh is, well, "chewy but flavorful" is about the best I can do. A nanny can be pretty good, but a billie is just plain tough. Goat is edible, especially if well-marinated, but it sure doesn't compare with mountain mutton!

Not only is their meat tough, but the goats are just plain tough critters. They also have a disastrous habit of heading for the ever-present precipice upon being threatened — including upon receiving a bullet. It's important to anchor a goat in his tracks, and you simply should not shoot if he's near a serious drop-off.

Goats are slab-sided creatures, and their toughness isn't so much physiological as mental. The answer is not hard bullets for extra penetration. Just the opposite, in fact; goats require bullets of appropriate deer/sheep calibers that are heavy enough to break bone but soft enough to expand readily and do damage. Shoot for the shoulder and don't hesitate to shoot again. If he can, a goat will dive for the nearest cliff with the last of his strength. At best he'll make recovery more difficult. At worst he'll ruin the horns and cape — or, worse yet, drop into a chasm where recovery is impossible. I've had two goats that were perfectly well-hit drop into chutes, but was lucky in that both hung up with no damage after short drops.

Something goat hunting has in common with sheep hunting is that it's classic mountain hunting offering a fine excuse to wander through some of the prettiest country on Earth. But goat hunting somehow lacks the snob appeal of sheep hunting. This means, whether for good reasons or bad, you needn't mortgage your home to hunt goats.

In the Lower 48 populations, permits are limited enough that drawing a tag is every bit as difficult as getting a sheep permit. There are exceptions; both Washington and Montana have a lot of goats, and some units aren't that hard to draw. But to plan a goat hunt without winning a permit draw you need to look farther north.

In both British Columbia and Alaska, nonresidents are obligated to hire a guide, which increases costs considerably. However, there's good news and more good news. First, due to inexplicably limited demand, guided goat hunts are quite reasonable, having escaped the runaway inflation of guided sheep hunts. Second, throughout most of B.C.'s mountain ranges and virtually all of southeast Alaska goats are an underhunted resource. Great billies die of old age each year — many, I suspect — without ever seeing a hunter. I hope it stays that way, for goat hunting is something I'd like to do more of while I've still got the legs and lungs for it. And not because it's a poor man's sheep hunt, but because the goat offers great hunting in his own right!

CHAPTER TEN ▪ PRONGHORN
Uniquely American and Totally Unique

PART GOAT, PART ANTELOPE, THIS UNIQUELY AMERICAN ANIMAL OFFERS ONE OF THE CONTINENT'S MOST ENJOYABLE HUNTING EXPERIENCES!

It's late November now and the fall is on the wane. A couple of late-season whitetail tags remain, but the season is pretty much gone. It's been a good year overall. Some good winter predator calling, a fine spring bear hunt. The summer doldrums were broken by an African hunt, and the fall schedule was a nice mix of country and game. Lord knows I can't complain – and yet something was missing. Interestingly, 1995 has been one of very few years in the last 30 that I didn't hunt the pronghorn antelope, still one of my favorite animals and most enjoyable hunts.

Part of it is the fact that the pronghorn was my very first big game animal. Most of us, I suspect, started with deer. But when I was growing up my home state of Kansas hadn't yet held her first modern hunting season. In those days Kansans were bird hunters, and those few who hunted big game simply had to travel out of state. A friend of Dad's, Jack Pohl of Bishop's Gunstocks in Warsaw, Missouri, hunted pronghorns in Wyoming every fall. Dad was a keen bird hunter and one of the finest wingshots I ever knew, but he never hunted big game. Pohl had taken both of us under his wing, teaching us about rifles and teaching me how to handload. Our final exam was to be a pronghorn hunt in Wyoming.

Just days before the long-awaited trip Jack fell off his horse and broke his ankle badly. His son, Henry, stood in and together we drove up to Gillette — with no place to hunt and no idea where to start looking. Dad stopped in the Gillette Chamber of Commerce. They recommended a full gas tank and some sandwiches, and suggested making a long circle through our hunting unit, stopping at every ranch until we found someone who would give us access. That was the day before the season, and of course we saw pronghorns everywhere. Pop wasn't a big game hunter,

perhaps a couple of other spots. These landowner tags can be costly since they're a sure thing. Otherwise, it's a take-your-chances lottery, with permits applied for in the late winter and spring. How tough the permits are to draw is generally a pure reflection of hunting pressure, trophy quality, or both. California, for instance, offers relatively few permits, residents only. The trophy quality is fabulous, but it can take a lifetime to draw. Arizona has easily the best pronghorns in North America, but permit numbers are low and the tags almost impossible to draw. Wyoming has far and away the most permits, but some units are almost "sure things" and others are very tough. The Red Desert region, for instance, is known as a great trophy-producing area, but permits are very hard to come by. Off on the east side, where I've done most of my hunting over the years, the country is mostly public land and the trophy quality is thought to be average. Drawing is usually easy.

The most overlooked pronghorn country is probably eastern Montana. There are loads of pronghorns and trophy quality is surprisingly good, but hunting pressure is low and chances for drawing very, very good. Colorado has limited numbers of pronghorns, but hunter interest is fairly low and the tags aren't all that hard to come by. Colorado also offers preference points, which makes drawing a tag eventually a sure thing.

Given a tag and a few days to hunt, a pronghorn hunt should be successful unless you're inordinately picky. I rarely am with pronghorns simply because I love to eat them as much as I like to hunt them. All my life I've had friends turn up their noses at pronghorns. Much as I hate to admit it, I have to concede that those first pronghorns Dad, Henry Pohl, and I shot were darn near inedible. I don't know exactly why, but I have some theories. Since I learned the hard way, I've skinned my pronghorns as quickly as possible, taking care to keep the hair off the meat and cooling them down as rapidly as I can. I also always bone the meat on the unproven theory that the bone marrow gives the strong taste. Handled quickly and properly, I'd rather have pronghorn than any other meat I know. No, it isn't like eating a sagebrush!

The other thing about trophy hunting for pronghorns is that few areas hold surprises. If you want big pronghorns, you need to be in an area that produces them. This is true with virtually every animal, but I find it especially true with pronghorns. In most areas the bucks are of a type; you can find one an inch or even two inches larger than the average if you look very hard. But in the typical pronghorn area that produces lots of 12 and 13 inch bucks you are very unlikely to find a 17 incher. Truth is most areas are managed too intensively to produce huge bucks — and in many areas pronghorn longevity is limited by bad winters.

For big pronghorns you need to look to areas with mild winters and limited permits. Northern Arizona and well-managed ranches in New Mexico are good bets. But, perhaps surprisingly, some of the highest percentages of very large pronghorns come out of eastern Oregon, northern California, and Nevada — all tough draw areas — and west Texas. Among areas that are accessible (meaning easy to draw) eastern Montana would be my top choice. Hunting pressure is light and the winters are generally surprisingly mild. My "best-ever" pronghorn came from West Texas, where the herd is small, but hunting pressure is light and the winters are mild, both factors combining to allow bucks to reach their full potential. My "second-best" pronghorn came from eastern Montana, which I consider an excellent and generally under-rated area. However, one should be mindful that Wyoming has the highest number of permits, the highest number of pronghorns, and consistently produces the largest number of Boone and Crockett heads. In terms of percentages the odds aren't high, but Wyoming does produce her share of monsters.

Generally speaking, after a day or so of scouting with good optics you should know what your area has to offer. If you're lucky enough to hit pronghorn country after a series of mild winters — two or three can make a big difference — then even so-so country can produce surprises.

Back in the '70s, after I got back from overseas with the Marines, Dad and I put in for pronghorn tags at Wright, Wyoming. We got there a day or so before the season and scouted around. That's the kind of country that usually produces lots of 13 inchers, but rarely better — under normal circumstances. While scouting Dad and I saw several nice bucks, but what I was seeing simply didn't register like it should have.

I spotted a very good buck with long prongs and horns that hooked sharply backwards — distinctive as well as nice. He was alongside a waterhole about two in the afternoon, and I decided he'd do just fine if I could find him in the morning. Of course he was there, in some hilly country about a half-mile from his water. He and his does drifted over about three hills, and I drifted with them, keeping low and closing the distance. I don't think it was yet eight a.m. when I shot him. He was as good as I'd thought, about 15-1/2 inches.

Through the day we saw a couple more good bucks that we couldn't get onto, but toward mid-afternoon a heavy-horned buck charged up out of a draw and insisted on filling Dad's tag. This one was actually a better buck than mine — a half-inch shorter, but much heavier all over. Both bucks measured over 80, certainly no mistakes. But with our tags filled, while we cruised around looking for prairie dog towns, we saw two or three bucks that were clearly bigger. There had been several mild winters, but I didn't appreciate the difference that made until that day. I appreciated it more the next year.

A buddy of mine, Tim Jones, and I came up the following year. He's a serious trophy hunter, so I'd filled him full of tales about the huge bucks we'd seen after we filled out. All they were was tales. The passing winter had been a hard one and the big bucks were simply gone. Plenty of pronghorn remained in their place, but all the bucks were of a type — 12 inches, maybe 13. We hunted hard for several days and never saw a buck close to 14! I think the older bucks go first in case of a hard winter or serious drought, but I also think a hard winter or very dry spring retards horn growth, just like it does on true antlered game.

Those horns that shed are just one of many unique features our *Antilocapra Americana* displays. His Latin name describes him as an antelope-goat, and indeed he has some characteristics of both types of ungulate. However, he is uniquely American and totally unique. His is a genus with just one species, and he has no close relatives anywhere in the world. He has coarse, hollow hair that provides superb insulation — hair unlike that of deer, goats, or antelope. He can hear reasonably well and probably has a decent sense of smell, but his first line of defense is his legendary eyes. Those orbs are set well apart, almost bug-eyed. Unlike many animals, you can't really move on a pronghorn when he's facing away or when his head is down feeding. He can almost see in a 360-degree circle, and it appears that his peripheral vision is as good as the rest. We simply don't know exactly how good those eyes are. I've often heard them compared to a man with 10-power binoculars, but I've read the same about sheep and deer. I tend to believe the pronghorn's vision is the

TOP: It's simply amazing what decoys can do — but unless you have total control over your hunting area this is not recommended for firearms hunters.
BOTTOM: Fort Belknap guide, Reno Shambo, Joe Healey, and Dwight van Brunt with Healey's pronghorn taken by using a decoy. It worked like a charm; Healey's buck darn near ran over the hunters!

best of all — and however good that is, suffice it to say that you simply cannot move around within sight of them and have any chance of closing within range.

I said a pronghorn's eyes were his first defense. That's not really true. The eyes are the warning system while the legs are really the defense. The pronghorn is built for speed, not only short bursts, but staying power. Those spindly-seeming leg bones have the strongest tensile strength in the animal kingdom, and that barrel-chested body is all lungs. For short bursts the pronghorn is almost as fast as the cheetah, but for the long haul nothing can touch him. When the eyes give warning he uses the legs — and he's gone from danger in a flash of buff and white, mouth open to suck in oxygen. When I was a kid all I ever saw was running pronghorns — and I supported the ammunition makers quite well trying to hit them. For many years now I've avoided shooting at running pronghorns like the plague. It can be done, but it's to be avoided — especially when they're running in a group. When I was a kid I gave the leading buck what I thought was a perfect lead — and cleanly dropped the doe two pronghorn behind him!

And yet pronghorn are hardly invulnerable. All too often hunters make the mistake of cruising pronghorn range in vehicles hoping to stumble onto one. That works. Worse yet, would-be hunters still chase them with vehicles in some areas. That works, too, but both solutions rob the pronghorn of his dignity as a game animal and cheat the hunter out of a truly fine experience. Stalking pronghorns is, to me, one of the most enjoyable hunts this continent offers. It can take time and sweat, and usually plenty of cactus spines, but is it fun!

That dead-flat, treeless country they inhabit usually isn't as dead-flat as it looks. There are usually unseen little gullies and rises that offer cover. If you spot your buck from afar, read the ground well, and take your time. It's amazing how close you can get. Sometimes.

Oddly, while pronghorn country may look all the same to you it doesn't to them. Pronghorns are surprisingly habitual in that featureless country. No, they don't use the same trails like whitetail. But if you spot one in a certain area at a certain time of day and you don't spook him unduly, chances are better than even he'll be in the same general area at the same time the next day. Certainly within a mile or less. He'll probably water at the same stock tank or pond at about the same time of day. And when pushed you can follow him for miles, but you'll often follow him along a circular path as he eventually heads back to the starting point.

On several occasions, after a couple failed stalks, I've given up on a particular buck late in the afternoon and found him the next morning close to where he was the first time I stalked him. And yet I don't think they move a great deal at night. If you find a buck towards last light and you don't think there's time remaining for a good stalk, you're almost better to leave him. Chances are good he'll be right there the next morning.

Last year I wanted to get a pronghorn for a young friend of mine, Adrian Flores. At 18 he'd been hunting for several seasons, but had been having terrible luck with deer and elk. I thought maybe pronghorn would change his luck, and I did everything I could to stack the deck. An outfitter friend of mine let me use part of his lease near Limon, Colorado, and we got tags for the right area. The problem was that, after a couple of scouting runs, I was pretty sure there was just one good buck in the area we had permission to hunt.

The day before the season Adrian met me in Limon and we went out to do one last scouting run — me hoping a couple of "backup bucks" had moved into the area. None had — and we also couldn't find the big one. I was frantic, because if he wasn't there our options were extremely limited in that private land-locked hunting unit. Just at dark he trooped up out of a little cut along a long ridge — the best place he could possibly be.

The next morning we left the truck well back on the far side of the ridge, hiked along below the skyline, and crawled over the top. As it usually is, the ground was more broken up close than it looked from afar — for several long, tense minutes we couldn't find them. Then I spotted a doe, and when we crawled farther we could see the whole herd.

Keeping low, we started down the ridge to close the distance just about the time the pronghorns started up the ridge. We met them head-on at a bit over 100 yards, and they almost caught us with our pants down. We had just time to get flat and get set up for a shot when the herd came into view, and Adrian took his first pronghorn very nicely with an easy shot well-executed. Me, well, I knew that was the only good buck in the pasture at that partic-ular time. So I did the sensible thing and shot the next young buck I saw. Sure was tasty!

I know that the does saw us on that occasion, but rather than spook they took a few steps forward for a closer look... and the buck followed suit, which was his undoing. This is not uncommon if you keep low, are perfectly still, and don't have anything unnatural such as glare from optics or a shiny riflestock. Pronghorn, I must admit, are not the brightest creatures on the planet. I think, as is the case with most animals, even their fabulous eyes key primarily on movement. And they have a healthy curiosity. The old timers used to "toll them in" by laying flat and raising a stick with a white flag. At a distance what we see of a pronghorn is a flash of white, and I expect that's also what they see, especially at long range. One might theorize that the pronghorn's reaction to a white flag isn't curiosity at all, but a response to a primitive decoy.

Whether that's true or not, decoying works. Boy, does it work! I do not recommend it for gun hunters, especially on public land. Hiding behind a pronghorn dummy just plain ain't smart! But for archers and hunters in unusually controlled situations it's extremely interesting to watch pronghorns react. I was up on the Fort Belknap Reservation in Montana with Dwight Van Brundt of Burris and *Outdoor Life*'s Joe Healey. It was late in the season and we were the only permit holders in the field, so we tried a decoy largely out of curiosity. Joe and our guide, Reno Shambo, pushed it ahead of them while stalking a nice buck. As soon as they came into view his reaction was instantaneous and startling — he darn near charged them! This decoy was a life-size image of a small buck. The rut was on and it was clear the large buck thought a youngster was horning in on his territory. Formerly the best tactic for archery was waiting at waterholes, but there's no doubt in my mind decoying is not only more effective but a lot more fun.

Depending on exactly where you are pronghorn generally rut late in September or very early in October. Most seasons are relatively short and specific, so you can't always pick the rut. While mating the bucks are more goofy than usual, which is good news, but the bad news is that they're almost constantly with a fairly large harem, which means there are a lot of eyes out there while you're stalking. Because of this, I don't think the exact time of the season is really important. In hard-hunted areas with short seasons, opening day is important. Actually, the couple of days prior is probably even more important. Half the hunt, especially if

TOP: Me and my father, Bud Boddington, made a nice double on these Montana pronghorn. Montana is under-rated as a pronghorn state, with good quality and an easy tag draw.
BOTTOM: My very best pronghorn was taken in West Texas. The herd is small there, but hunting pressure is light and winters mild, so bucks grow to full potential.

you're seeking a trophy buck, is finding one and figuring out where he lives and how to waylay him. This is best done before hunting pressure shifts things around.

In areas with longer seasons, say 10 days or more, the end of the season can actually be as good as the opener. Most prong-horn pressure occurs on opening day, and the animals can get pretty stirred up. The pressure curve drops swiftly, and after a few days things settle back to normal. But do be aware that pronghorns drop their horns quite early.

The horns — cognified epithelium, like finger nails, with some hair enclosed, especially at the base — grow up around a bony core. Unique in the animal kingdom, they're shed annually with the shedding usually taking place in mid-November. New growth starts very soon after and continues through the winter and spring. Eastern Montana is one of the places with a long pronghorn season. It starts early in October, before deer season, then continues on through much of the deer season, making a combo hunt possible. By the end of the season, usually mid-November, a great percentage of the bucks have lost their horns, making for slim pickings. One year, very late in the season, Jack Atcheson Jr. and I glassed a massive group of pronghorns way out on a sagebrush flat. This, too, is typical of pronghorns — after mating season and as winter approaches they congregate into huge herds, almost certainly so they can collectively stamp through the snow to feed.

There were just a few bucks in the herd — easily 100 animals — that still had horns, and one was clearly outstanding. There was just one way to get close enough, and that was to crawl — a long, long distance. After an eternity of getting cactus spines in our knees, hands, and elbows, we closed the range to long shoot-ing distance. Jack led the way to a particularly tall sagebrush clump and we set up the spotting scope so we could be sure we had the right buck. Right there, while we watched, he dropped his head to feed and came up with just one horn! After all that crawling I was happy to settle for second best, a nice buck, but nothing like the one that got away!

Pronghorn hunting is mostly a game for good optics, good stalking, and plenty of patience. The optics are absolutely essen-tial, for it's critical that pronghorn first be spotted as far away as possible and also judged for quality if that is important to you. Pronghorns are quite difficult to judge, and at first they all look bigger than they are. The ears are about six inches from butt to tip, which is a good indicator. What's hard to see is how much the horns curl in or back at the tip. A pronghorn that doubles the ears is a 12-inch buck, but the tips can add three inches or more if they hook sharply and well. Good binoculars backed up with a spotting scope are really essential. Once a decision is reached, good stalking and patience take over.

In my experience it's a myth that pronghorns must be taken at long range. Without a doubt ranges average longer than with most big game animals, but only once have I taken a pronghorn at more than 400 yards, and very few over 300. On that same Fort Belknap hunt — where you can purchase two tags — I decided to take my second buck with Dwight's XP-100 pistol in 7mm-08. I shot it and figured I was good to 200 yards, hoping for half that. Reno Shambo and I followed a buck into some broken ground where a plateau fell off into ravine-cut badlands. The buck decided to come up the same ridge we were coming down, and we had a meeting engagement at point-blank range. At about 30 yards all I could see through the handgun scope was hair, fortunately the right hair in the right spot.

I expect the average shot is somewhere on the near side of 200 yards. This means ultra-long-range rigs really aren't essential. However, accuracy is important because the pronghorn presents a relatively small target. A flat-shooting rifle is important, too, because range is very difficult to judge in that open country. Best to have a rifle that shoots flat enough so you can hold in the center of the chest at moderate ranges and high on the shoulder if he looks kinda small. Magnum power is not needed, but a pronghorn's stamina shouldn't be under-rated. Hit well, no problem, but hit poorly and a pronghorn can lead you on a very long day.

If you're a good and patient stalker and the country is relatively broken a .243 or 6mm are just fine, but if you need to take shots beyond 250 yards or so you're pushing the energy envelope. To my mind, the perfect pronghorn caliber is the .25-06, with the good old .270 Winchester an equally sound second choice. Of course, any flat-shooting deer caliber will do just fine, and there's nothing wrong with the small belted cartridges like the .240, .257, and .270 Weatherby, and the .264 Winchester Magnum.

The wind-swept sagebrush hills and open prairies the pronghorn calls home are uniquely beautiful in their way — and the pronghorn is one of the most strikingly handsome animals in the world. Especially in terms of sheer enjoyment, hunting him is also one of the most underrated pastimes in the hunting world. I really missed crawling through the cactus after him this year, and that's a mistake I hope I don't repeat soon!

CHAPTER ELEVEN ■ MULE DEER
Where Have All the Mule Deer Gone?

THE GREAT DAYS OF MULE DEER HUNTING ARE OVER, BUT THERE ARE STILL GREAT MULE DEER... IF YOU KNOW WHERE TO LOOK.

Dark was falling quickly, but not as quickly as the freezing rain mixed with thick, wet snowflakes. I was driving through northern Utah, and I happened to glance to the left at a little stock tank nestled in a sagebrush coulee. Just on the far side of the tank was a huge mule deer, the kind you dream of — thick, dark antlers, spreading wide and with clean, deep forks. The Utah season had just ended, and I was glad to see this buck. Glad that he had survived, and glad that his classic mule deer habitat still held such bucks. Unfortunately great bucks like him are no longer common today — certainly not in the Rocky Mountain high country, the core of what has always been the most classic mule deer range.

It's hard to define exactly what many like to refer to as "The Golden Age of Mule Deer Hunting," but for darn sure I missed it. The best years varied with the area, and the downhill slide was almost imperceptible at first. The early 1960s were probably the peak for trophy mule deer hunting across most of the West, but some traditional trophy country remained fabulous well into the 1970s. I could have gotten in on the bonanza, but mule deer weren't a big thing to me 30 years ago. I was much more interested in elk hunting and saving up for a first African hunt; I never even attempted to hunt trophy mule deer until it was much too late.

The perception back then was that all you needed to do to bag a heavy-beamed 30-inch mule deer was show up in the right area and look around a bit. Chances are it was never quite that easy, but there was some reality in this perception. The Rocky Mountain West, the core mule deer range, was lightly inhabited and lightly hunted back then. Ski slopes and condominiums were few, mineral exploration was light, and elk numbers were low. While management manipulations have kept overall numbers high in many areas, the percentage of mature and old bucks that existed just a few decades ago will never be seen again.

In those days serious mule deer hunters had it good — and many of them now in their 50s and 60s still have the big racks to prove it. Nonresident hunters in numbers were a new facet of a more affluent and mobile post-war America. Casinos all across Nevada hosted "big buck" contests (some still do), and merchants all through the Rockies welcomed the hordes of hunters from the East and West Coast. Even the game managers got in on a little free enterprise; Utah was not alone, but she was a prime example of selling her deer herd. During the Golden Age you could fill a tag and go buy another... and another.

The decline was not an avalanche, but a slow downhill slide that continues to this day across the heart of the Rockies. Season by season the mature mossy-horned bucks became ever more scarce — and in many areas overall numbers have followed suit.

The reasons are not altogether understood — and since the cause is uncertain, the solution is less so. Part of the problem, especially in the reduction of mature, trophy-class bucks, has been overhunting, but only part. Human development, whether mineral, recreational, or urban sprawl, has blocked or destroyed much critical winter range. Then there are various experts' pet theories: sagebrush eradication, unchecked increases in predators, the elk population explosion. Sometimes disease is a factor, like the chronic wasting disease that is a serious current problem. All have validity, with the real reason probably resting in some combination of factors depending on the area. Add drought or a killer winter to several of these other factors and you have a disaster requiring years to recover from.

A large part of the problem is politics. Thanks to those long lines of out-of-state autos (whose occupants aren't so welcome any more, but whose dollars are) that converge on mule deer country each fall, mule deer became a cash crop with politicians unwilling to do anything that might interrupt the cash flow. But ever so slowly the reins have tightened. Arizona was the first western state to institute across-the-board deer tags-by-drawing. Wyoming and Nevada followed. Idaho and Montana established quotas. Several years ago, in an extremely unpopular, downright courageous, and absolutely essential move, Utah went to across-the-board drawings. Colorado finally crossed this inevitable line as well.

Limited permits are the present and future of mule deer hunting. It is unlikely to ever get easier to get a tag — especially in a good area. Nor is it likely to get cheaper. The new wave is to make more expensive tags more available — and not only on private land. In a weak moment I paid $500 for a "sure thing" 1996 Montana deer license, which makes one wonder where it can go. At least the tag drawings are fair to all, and they work. Nevada's trophy bucks were badly depleted when she went to tag drawings, but in just a few years bucks of "4x4" or better formed the majority of the harvest. Drought has had its impact recently, but Nevada — seldom considered a hotspot in the "Golden Age" — remains fine trophy country today. I expect much of the traditional trophy country in both Utah and Colorado to recover, at least to some degree, given time and a conservative buck harvest.

Right now, however, and almost certainly for a long time to come, I consider a really large trophy mule deer — not necessarily a "book" deer, but a buck with mass, length, points, character, and class — the most difficult trophy in North America. It takes luck and persistence, but there are many places to bag a great whitetail. The way elk herds are exploding new elk hotspots are emerging every year. Sheep hunting generally means either an expensive hunt or beating the odds in a tough draw, but with enough money and/or a great tag wonderful sheep can be taken. Even with a great tag in the best remaining areas there are no assurances of a great mule deer.

And what are the best areas? Within "traditional" trophy mule deer country, roughly from the eastern front of the Rockies westward to the Sierras, there are very few hotspots. The remote Arizona Strip country, almost impossible to get into, still holds monsters among its few deer. Arizona's Kaibab Plateau, though weather-dependent, continues to yield giants. Likewise Utah's Paunsaugant Plateau, though perhaps it's even more weather-sensitive. These are all permit areas, tough to draw (or, in the case of some Paunsaugant landowner tags, pricey).

New Mexico's Jicarilla Apache Reservation, also expensive, continues to produce some giant mulies. Nevada shouldn't be overlooked. Especially in western Nevada the buck/doe ratios are extremely high, genetics are superb, and the age class distribution is good. Southern Idaho was a real hotspot a few years ago. Notoriety and some bad winters have had impact, but good trophy potential remains.

Mind you, big mule deer are where you find them. The odd giant still turns up in western Colorado or western Wyoming, and that buck I saw in northern Utah was wonderful, but these days such bucks are increasingly few and far between. Fortunately the mule deer situation is a good deal brighter in many non-traditional and fringe areas. Perhaps only coincidentally, these are almost universally areas where elk are not a factor.

Mule deer are making and have made a wonderful comeback on the southern Great Plains, at least some of it due to carefully controlled permits. It's a closely-guarded local secret, but western Kansas is producing some huge mule deer these days. Unfortunately this is mostly a playground for Kansas residents; the only nonresident tags in the best mule deer country are archery or muzzleloader.

Almost as good, and much more accessible, are the plains units in eastern Colorado. These are all draw units, with the best-known areas, such as the famed Purgatory in southern Colorado, requiring several preference points. But today you could encounter a monster mulie almost anywhere in eastern Colorado — and many of the units are a one-point or no-point draw.

I spent several falls both hunting and guiding in eastern Colorado, and it was very interesting. Our primary quarry was usually whitetail, but the mule deer were amazing. Many of us used to be concerned that whitetail would push the mule deer out — and this seemed to be happening in many areas. But at least in some of Colorado's high plains the two species seem to be making peace with each other. One property we hunted is cut but by a winding north-south cottonwood-lined watercourse. Whitetails frequent the northern half, while the southern part of drainage is almost all mule deer. Go figure!

It used to be that almost all hunting pressure in the region was on the more visible, more vulnerable mule deer. The current interest in trophy whitetails has actually taken a lot of pressure off the mule deer. On that particular ranch we posted a hunter overlooking a big hayfield one evening, and by last light he had 52 mule deer, including 14 bucks, in front of him!

Shooting is often fairly long in good mule deer country. Learning to find and use a natural rest — quickly — as well as good range estimation are critical skills, especially for trophy bucks.

An outfitter friend of mine, Mike Watkins, hunts country in northeastern Wyoming, southeastern Montana, and southwestern South Dakota. I've hunted with him a number of times — in all three states. All have an interesting mixture of whitetail and mule deer, but the mule deer are generally more numerous and there are good numbers of genuinely mature bucks throughout this region. Plains mule deer are typically smaller and lighter-antlered than the classic high country bucks, but given the chance to reach full maturity they can be exceptional. In the last few years I've seen great bucks by almost anyone's standard. Perhaps more importantly, I've seen lots of nice, mature bucks that most of us would be very happy with.

Back in Colorado, but farther west along the foothills of the Rocky Mountain Front, the mule deer numbers are also very high. Much of this country is highly developed, a unique situation that I call "urban mule deer." A friend of mine, Boulder attorney and outfitter Lad Shunneson, has leased and hunted a smallish ranch north of Boulder for many years. Houses have sprung up around and even on it, but that place remains the darndest buck funnel I've ever seen. Especially late in the season you can see big bucks — and different bucks — every morning and evening.

There are also some superb mule deer both north and south of what we think of as mule deer country. To the north, mule deer are coming back nicely in southwestern Alberta. This is undoubtedly due to limited outfitter permits and the current emphasis on whitetail hunting, but whatever the reason, given the chance to mature those Canadian mule deer grow huge.

The other oddball option is to the south, technically in desert mule deer country (subspecies *Odocoileus hemionus crooki*). Desert mule deer are smaller in body, but they can grow huge antlers depending on local food and genetics, and whether they're left alone long enough. The situation is uneven, but I've seen great bucks in southern Arizona, southern New Mexico,

TOP: Terry Moore and I took these bucks on the same morning in western South Dakota. The Great Plains is one of very few areas where mule deer are increasing in numbers, although monsters are rare there are good numbers of mature bucks.
BOTTOM: In January 2002, hunting with Ernesto Zaragoza's Solimar Safaris, I took my first and only mule deer that reaches the magical 30-inch spread that mule deer hunters crave. He's a beautiful buck, but spread is just one measurement — he could be heavier and needs better point length to score well!

and in west Texas as far east as Midland. Without question, however, the biggest desert mule deer — and some of the biggest mule deer currently available to hunters — come out of Sonora in Old Mexico.

Due to high demand and increasingly limited permits, this is an expensive deer hunt today, on a par with the Jicarilla or a private Paunsaugant permit. It is also not a sure thing; there aren't many deer and the shooting is difficult, but the potential is fabulous. One of my best mule deer in terms of score came out of Sonora in the early '90s, and in January 2002 I took my first mule deer that achieved the magical "30-inch spread" that we all dream about.

This is a tracking hunt, and the Mexican cowboys are the best trackers I've ever seen — even better than the rightfully legendary African trackers. The desert floor, where the deer live, is brushy; the shooting is fast and quick decisions are essential. The trackers are great, but usually don't speak much English — so you must be prepared to make up your own mind. Quickly. If you're lucky you'll shoot your buck in his bed, but more likely you'll shoot him, or shoot at him, as he bobs and weaves through mesquite and cholla. Expect a chance at one great buck in a week's hard hunting.

Like most great hunts this is not a sure thing. Hunting with various outfitters, I've taken three bucks in Sonora out of five hunts. This is pretty good, actually. In January 2002, hunting with Ernesto Zaragoza's Solimar Safaris, we had six hunters in camp and we took seven mule deer (tags are private land tags, and a second buck is legal if tags are available) and two Coues' deer. One buck, taken by Dwight Van Brunt, was spectacular. My 30-inch buck was good, and three other bucks were fully mature, heavy-antlered "keepers." There were two mistakes, medium-sized bucks that should have been allowed to grow up, but things happen fast in the brushy desert, and sometimes you don't get as good a look as you need.

Many hunters have concerns about travel in Mexico, but generally without justification. If you book with a good outfitter and follow his advice you should have no trouble. I've made many trips down there for both mule deer and Coues' deer, and I've never had any problems.

We've covered my spin on the "where" of big mule deer today, but what is a big buck? Mule deer hunters, like moose hunters, talk about spread, but this is just one measurement. My 2002 Sonora buck was a typical four-by-four with eyeguards, decent points, good beam length, medium mass, and an outside spread of 31 inches. You wouldn't pass him any-where, but my buddy Dwight Van Brunt's buck, taken on the same trip, was much better in almost all ways. His buck had more massive antlers, longer beams, and deeper forks and is a classic "190 B&C" buck. Mine doesn't come close — but my buck is a "30-incher," while his has a spread of "only" 28 inch-es. Take your pick.

Thirty-inch bucks exist, but they aren't common — and spread isn't necessarily the most important factor if you're into record-book score. Mass and tine length count more, score-wise, and to my eye are more impressive. But the wonderful thing about trophy deer is that no two racks are alike, and beauty is in the eye of the beholder.

Whether you're a "spread freak" or not, the 30-inch mule deer is scarce nowadays — as are bucks that are big in all the other dimensions. These days a mature buck of 4-1/2 years or more with good mass, reasonable points, and a spread of 24 to 26 inches is a very fine buck. The chances are so slim today for a buck that will reach the Boone and Crockett minimum that I consider it foolish to even hunt for such a beast — unless you're prepared for lots of disappointment, and of course unless you gain access to one of the few magical, mystical, and almost mythical hotspots.

Keep in mind that the vast majority of mule deer that do reach that wondrous score of 190 fall short of the 30-inch mark. Only three of the current "top 15" mule deer in the Boone and Crockett record book have an inside spread exceeding 30 inch-es — and the Number 15 typical mule deer, taken by Wesley Brock in Grand County, Colorado (in 1963, clearly a "Golden Age" buck), has an inside spread of just 21 4/8 inches!

But regardless of how they get there, mule deer that grow 190-plus inches of antler are both awesome and rare — whether you speak of gross or net. Unless you already have very nice mule deer trophies, an unlimited budget, an aversion to venison, or you like punishment, set your sights 10 to 20 inches lower today — and hope Lady Luck smiles.

After the "where" and "what" we should discuss "how." This has not changed much. Except in special circumstances like heavy oak brush or Sonora's mesquite desert, mule deer are far more visible than their whitetail cousins. Glassing is generally the best technique, with early morning and late evening the most active periods. Mule deer are not as difficult to hunt as whitetails. The problem with big mule deer today isn't that they've gotten more wary — it's that there simply aren't as many! However, the survivors, the ones that have lived to full maturity and grown those legendary antlers, aren't exactly the pushovers of the 1960s. And, no, they don't always stop to look back.

A couple of years ago outfitter Mike Watkins and I drove into a new ranch that was supposed to have some great deer. At dawn, enroute to the ranch house to "check in," we passed a hayfield that was full of mule deer — mostly bucks. There were several "keepers," nice plains deer, but we weren't too excited — until we glassed a big-bodied buck at the far end of the field.

Oh, my! He was well outside his ears, very high, and very heavy. He was looking right at us, so we couldn't count points. I assume he was a 4x4 plus eyeguards (which we could see), but he might have had small kickers. Whatever he was, he was a mid-180s frame, minimum, and if he had deep forks he was 10 inches better at least. He was the best mule deer I'd seen in quite a long time, and he was mine.

He was about 450 yards, but I had a laser range finder and a .300 Weatherby that would reach him. We never considered this most obvious option. We also never considered one of us staying to watch him. We had permission, so we could have done either. Instead, at my insistence, we played the game properly and went on to the house, said our "hello's," and launched a stalk around the back side of the field, which should have brought us to within 200 yards of the buck's last known location.

We made the circle with the wind good, then crept up to the ridge overlooking the field. About the time we got there deer started to trickle out of the field, finished with their morning feeding. We viewed the procession for an hour, but the big buck was not among them. Non-plussed, we climbed to a high ridge that overlooked the field and system of sagebrush draws beyond. We had no trouble picking out the bedded forms of numerous deer, or recognizing deer we'd seen in the field and leaving the field, but the big boy was simply gone, and we never saw him again. So much for stupid mule deer.

The best technique for mule deer is to get high and get comfortable and spend your time glassing with good optics. At any

My buddy, Dwight Van Brunt, took this mule deer in Sonora, Mexico in January 2002. This is one of the prettiest and most perfect mule deer I have ever seen, "just" 28 inches wide, but heavy throughout, even, and carrying excellent point length.

time of the season this is the best technique to locate a big buck. Obviously the chances are best during the rut, when even the older, more sedentary bucks are far more active and visible. In fact, a trick the late Jerry Hughes, a great Nevada outfitter, taught me is that during the rut you don't even worry about finding bucks. Glass up a group of does and stay with them — for days if necessary. Sooner or later a big buck will show up. By the way, if the country is such that glassing is not an option, then the rut is not necessarily the best time to hunt. In Mexico, for instance, the cowboys can pick up good tracks at any time during the season, but during the rut the bucks are travelling, and they will generally have to follow them much farther. In tracking, the longer you must follow a track before the buck beds, the better the chance of losing the track. Even without tracking, prior to the rut bucks are much more habitual and easier to figure out — if you can find them — but when the rut occurs all bets are off.

Mexico and some of the thick oak-brush country are exceptions. In the main, mule deer are open-country animals, generally visible and usually fairly vulnerable. If you can find them. The trick is to hunt where they are, meaning where the kind of buck you desire is present. Hunt patiently and with good optics and reasonable expectations. When you see something you like, move in decisively with cover between you and the animal and the wind in your favor. And don't expect him to look back!

CHAPTER TWELVE ■ MOOSE
The World's Largest Deer

SOMETIMES COMICAL, OCCASIONALLY DANGEROUS, AND ALWAYS MAGNIFICENT, THE MOOSE IS THE KING OF ALL ANTLERED GAME.

A number of years ago, while hunting Dall's sheep in Alaska's Wrangell Mountains, my guide and I took a much-needed breather on a little bench cut on a steep shale mountainside. The nearest scrub timber was far below, and the only vegetation was a bit of grass that managed to creep through the mossy rocks. There on that bench was the bleached skull and antlers of a good-sized bull moose. All other bones were long gone. Whatever drama had occurred here had taken place in the late winter; one antler had been neatly shed, while the other remained attached to the skull.

I have thought about that bull moose for many years, wondering what possessed him to climb so far above his sheltered valley, and how he met his end on that bleak mountain. Probably he was harried by wolves, or perhaps he was trying to escape unusually deep snows. Or maybe he just wanted to see what lay on the other side and didn't quite make it. But one thing is sure about moose — you can't figure them out. Just when you think they're an over-sized, amiable, and not-too-bright deer they will surprise you.

Twenty-some years ago, when I was going through the riverine portion of the Army's Mountain Warfare School at Fort Greeley, Alaska, our boat came around a sharp bend in the Tanana River. A bull moose stood in the calmer water on the inside of the turn — except we didn't know he was a bull. The water rose nearly to his belly, and his outstretched neck — head, ears, and antlers — were totally submerged as he nibbled on some underwater succulents. We floated to within a few yards before the head came up — and the wall of water he threw in his hasty departure nearly capsized us.

In retrospect slipping up on that moose may not have been the smartest thing I ever did. I'm not one of those writers who places

or an open hillside where a stalk would be possible. But on this last day of the season there was no tomorrow. And besides that, it was far too cold to wait all day. So we got the wind right and edged slowly into the timber. Along the way we bumped a couple of cows, but our luck held. The big bull stood up at 60 yards, and then the work began.

Although there may be options I'm not aware of, the techniques for hunting moose are generally glassing, still-hunting, and calling. My preference is far and away glassing — finding a good vantage point and working the binoculars until something interesting is located, then planning a stalk. A moose is a very large animal. Not only that, but his black color stands out... and on a sunny day his white or golden antlers will catch the light and gleam at incredible distances. There are just two problems with glassing for moose. First, you can often see moose so far away that you have absolutely no chance of getting to them, at least not on that day, and you may have less chance of being able to pack a bull out if you can get to him. Second, you must have terrain relief in order to glass.

Moose are creatures of the northern forests, with strong preference for swampy country with willow and alder. If there are hills and valleys and meadows you can glass. However, in heavily forested country or relatively flat boggy stuff — which comprises a great deal of moose country — you may not have the vistas you need for glassing. Still-hunting, cruising good areas and looking for moose, is a viable option. But moose are big animals and need a lot of country, so such hunting can be a lot like looking for a needle in a haystack even where there are lots of moose. A better wrinkle is to still-hunt lakeshores from a canoe, or by floating along a northern river. You need to cover a lot of ground to bump into a big bull moose.

For this reason calling is generally the method of choice in level country with a lot of forest. Especially in country where moose have just as much trouble seeing other moose as you have seeing them, moose respond quite readily to calling. The sound is a deep, guttural grunting, traditionally rendered from a rolled-up "loudspeaker" of birchbark. It works and is perhaps

TOP: Packing moose is just plain hard work. How much you can carry depends not only on your condition, but also on the terrain and the distance you must carry it. Few can pack out a moose in less than eight loads.
BOTTOM: My best moose was taken on the Alaskan Peninsula. This is a heavy-horned old giant, with very wide palms and lots of mass everywhere. He was stalked in his bed and shot at very close range.

the most exciting way to hunt moose. Especially since it works best during the rut, when a wild-eyed moose is likely to come rushing in amid a crashing of brush.

The problem with calling moose is that it's like most other options for calling in game: calling moose is rut-dependent, making the right time difficult to pick for visiting sportsmen. And if you're trophy hunting there may not be a lot of time to properly evaluate the antlers before you must shoot or lose the opportunity.

I prefer glassing, with the understanding that it isn't practical everywhere. Glassing for moose is a bit different than with many species. Simply seeing the moose isn't the problem. Sometimes they appear out of nowhere, having stood up from a bed or stepped out of heavy brush, but more often they stick out like sore thumbs. The problem is finding them once you get there.

The best moose I ever shot or am likely to shoot was a classic example. We were on the Alaska Peninsula, and we'd seen a couple of bulls but nothing dramatic. My guide, Chris Kempf, recalled a huge bull he'd seen the year before in a little valley a couple of miles away. So we hiked that way and set up on a low ridge that overlooked a willow-choked basin a good half-mile across. We glassed for a long time and saw no moose. Then Chris spotted an antler sticking up in the willows right below us.

The bull was bedded tight with just his antlers sticking up. After long deliberation we agreed he was about 325 yards away, an acceptable shooting distance, yet not an easy shot, especially with the strong and gusty crosswind, but there was nothing to shoot at. We decided to let the moose make the first move; perhaps he would offer a good shot where he was, or perhaps he would move to a better spot. We waited for a half-hour, then an hour, and nothing happened. Then we decided to go in after him.

We marked his position as best we could, dropped off the ridge and moved downwind to circle in on him. We stumbled around in that willow jungle for nearly an hour, and the moose simply wasn't there. He must have gotten up and moved, so we backed out of the tangle and climbed back up on the ridge to relocate him.

Nope, hadn't moved. He was still in exactly the same place in exactly the same position, and we'd just plain overshot him. So we took new bearings and went in again, shooting him as he jumped from his bed at 20 yards.

Outfitter Toby Johnson and I had a similar situation when I

drew a Shiras moose permit in Wyoming's Bighorn Mountains, but this time the problem was fog. Toby knew of a very good bull living in a wonderful alder basin, and had scouted out the perfect vantage point to glass him from. Except the basin remained completely cloaked in dense fog the first two days of my hunt. Once, out of sheer boredom and frustration, we blundered in there anyway to try to find him. After bumping several cows we came to our senses, considered ourselves lucky, and backed off. On the third day it cleared, and we spotted the bull lying in a little meadow. We marked the spot well, crawled in on him, and I shot him.

The moose, good old *Alces alces*, is the largest living member of the deer family. He is not strictly a North American mammal; his tribe circumnavigates the globe in the Northern Hemisphere and is found in several subspecies throughout the northern forests. The very largest moose, in both body and antler, are found in extreme northwestern Canada and Alaska, what we call the Alaska-Yukon moose.

Now that eastern Siberia, once a sensitive area for military reasons, is open to outsiders, it has been discovered that this part of Russia produces moose that are every bit as big as those in Alaska. On a bear hunt in Kamchatka, I measured a Siberian moose that had an honest-to-gosh spread of 70 inches — and everything else to go with it. Don't start packing your bags just yet. There are big moose in Siberia, but my impression is that the population is thinly scattered, with the better hunting still remaining on the U.S. side of the pond. Moving west from Siberia, the size of moose drops off quickly until you get to the small moose (locally called "elg," which is where our term "elk" comes from) of Scandinavia. The European moose are generally smaller than our own Shiras moose. To some degree this is a function of management. Finland has the most dense moose population in the world, and the harvest, though carefully controlled, is intense. European moose are probably a smaller subspecies than our Shiras and eastern moose, but once in a while a specimen is taken with antlers large enough to make you wonder.

In North America size generally drops off as you move east. The Canada moose — including both *A. a. andersoni* from the Mackenzie River and British Columbia east to the Great Lakes; and *americanus* from the Great Lakes east to Newfoundland and New England — is definitely a smaller moose than the Alaska-Yukon moose (*A.a. gigas*). The moose of northern British Columbia are clearly the largest of the Canada moose, but it's obvious that at some point this population starts to transition to the Alaska-Yukon variety. With Canada moose elsewhere, however, size may be a function of management. The reopening of Maine moose hunting produced so many record-class bulls that it's no longer clear, at least not to me, that eastern moose are smaller than the moose of, say, Alberta or Manitoba. Newfoundland, although generally managed for quantity rather than quality, produces some real whoppers every year.

The smallest North American moose are the Shiras or Wyoming moose, a small, very dark moose that is still a monster of a deer. A mature Shiras bull moose should weigh around 900 to 1,000 pounds. A good Canada moose bull should be 300 pounds or so heavier, and an Alaska-Yukon bull can top three-quarters of a ton. And of course there are tremendous variances among individuals.

Antler size differentiation is more clear cut. Like all antlered game, there are numerous aspects to a moose rack that the serious trophy hunter must understand and learn to study — quickly. Number of points, height and width of palms, presence and size of brow palms — all of these things are extremely important in a final trophy measurement, if that matters to you. However, sort of like elk hunters talk about numbers of points (as in "six-by-six") and bear hunters talk about squared measurements (as in "nine-foot bear"), moose hunters talk first and most about spread. Remembering that spread is just one element in an official score, spread is an easy approach to moose trophy quality. With Alaska-Yukon moose, a 60-inch bull is good. With Canada moose, a 50-inch bull is good. With Shiras moose, a 40-inch bull is good. Add five inches to any of these measurements and you can say "very good." Add 10 inches and you can say "wonderful."

And having said that, big moose are becoming very difficult prizes these days. There are several reasons. One that will come and go periodically is bad winters. Another that is becoming worse is an increase in wolves, which has seriously knocked moose populations in many areas. Yet another is that trophy moose hunting has received a great deal more attention in recent years. Due to

TOP: My favorite moose-hunting technique is glassing. The big, dark animals usually stand out at great distances, with the biggest problem seeing moose but finding them again when you stalk them.
BOTTOM: The preference point system works, especially if you get in on the ground floor. In 1999, I drew a Shiras moose permit in Wyoming's Bighorn Mountains, where I took this excellent bull with outfitter Toby Johnson.

this latter factor there aren't as many untouched hotspots as there used to be. And because of the first two, there aren't as many places producing big moose as there used to be.

For big Alaskan moose, I'd look to the southwestern approaches to the Brooks Range, where there is still very little resident pressure. On a recent spring bear hunt I saw literally hundreds of moose along willow-lined rivers — the most I have ever seen anywhere. Western Alaska is good, and don't overlook the Mackenzie District of Northwest Territories. The outfitters there have long overlooked their moose due to emphasis on sheep and the logistics involved with recovering moose. But due to increased demand they're looking a lot harder at their moose, and they're pulling out some monsters.

For the best Canada moose the record books are pretty clear, with northern B.C. dominating the listings. However, that isn't the only place. Northern Alberta is overlooked and under-rated, and northern Manitoba is another sleeper. For those who aren't quite so trophy conscious, the most enjoyable moose hunting I know of — and probably the most successful — is Newfoundland. Success rates are extremely high due to a huge moose population, and while average antler size is small there can be some surprises. In 2003, hunting Newfoundland's northern peninsula with Mobile Outfitters, my hunting partner, John Chaves, and I both took beautiful bulls over 50 inches in spread.

Shiras moose are best hunted wherever you can draw a tag, although Utah and Wyoming tend to have the edge in trophy quality. After many years of applying I finally drew the Wyoming tag I mentioned earlier, and I took a very fine Shiras moose. I have also hunted this small, dark type of moose twice in the Kootenays of southeastern B.C. Years ago I gave up arguing where the line should be drawn. It has to be drawn somewhere, and from a record-keeping standpoint the U.S.-Canada border makes sense, but southeastern B.C.'s moose are much more like Shiras than Canadian moose. Whatever you call them, hunting moose in the mountains, whether the Canadian or the U.S. Rockies, was quite a lot different from hunting them in the boggy valleys to the north. Shiras moose are hunted more like elk, and it is a most enjoyable experience.

Although a very large and strong animal, I haven't found moose to be as hardy as elk when it comes to choosing rifles and cartridges. They are, however, different. Moose seem impervious to

A good Alaska-Yukon moose. This bull was glassed at long range, then stalked into heavy timber. The spread is about 65 inches.

bullet shock; I don't think you can impress them with foot-pounds or velocity. On the other hand, they don't seem to have the elk's tendency to travel for miles and miles with a slightly off-center hit. A moose is as likely as not to show no reaction what-soever to a very good hit, and walk or trot into heavy cover and fall over.

I have shot moose with the .338 Winchester Magnum, the .340 Weatherby Magnum, the .375 H&H Magnum, and the .416 Remington Magnum. I don't necessarily think such cannons are called for. I have also used the .35 Whelen and the little .358 Winchester. Both worked perfectly, and I absolutely believe in heavy, large-caliber bullets for game this large. However, my Dad, shooting his .308 Winchester, absolutely flattened a big bull in his tracks. Go figure.

One time I shot a smallish bull at fairly long range with a .340 Weatherby Magnum, hardly a pipsqueak cartridge. He was stand-ing on a little ridge across a willow bog, and I was certain I had the hold right. I shot three times, each time believing I could hear the bullet hit. After the third shot the bull walked out of sight behind some willows. Which is exactly where we found him, with a very nice three-shot group on his shoulder. This is not unusual.

Another time I was sitting on a knife-edge ridge looking down at a narrow timbered creek. A good bull walked almost directly under me, and I shot him just beside the spine and down through heart and lungs with a .338 shooting a 250-grain Trophy Bonded Bearclaw. This was a devastating hit with a devastating bullet. But there was no visible reaction other than the bull launching into a run, then piling up in 30 yards.

Based on experiences like these, I believe the sheer size of a moose demands heavy-for-caliber bullets with good penetrating qualities. But I've given up on the idea that I can flatten a moose with heavy artillery. I'd have perfect confidence in a .30-06 with a good 180-grain bullet, and I'd be much more likely to use a .270 or 7mm on moose than I would on elk.

A point of departure between moose hunting and most other North American hunting is the sheer logistics involved with pack-ing out a moose. Nowhere is it more true that the work begins after the shooting is over! Although it's somewhat true with elk, it is absolutely true with moose that you simply have to be care-ful where you shoot one. Not only in terms of shot placement, but where on the ground the moose is located.

We can talk macho all we want about being able to pack any-thing out of anywhere, but packing out a moose will take even the best man at least six trips. More like eight. If you can't get him out — before the meat spoils — then you can't shoot him. This from a practical legal standpoint as well as the more important ethical consideration. Over the years, at speaking engagements and in casual conversations, I have increasingly discouraged unguided moose hunting for this simple reason. Unless you have the logistics completely figured out before you squeeze the trigger, you're a walking game violation.

That is one of the biggest differences between a guided hunt and an unguided hunt; a guide who intends to stay in business will have the logistics figured. It may be horses, it may be an Argo or other tracked vehicle, or it may be a lot of man hours for you and your guide, but it will happen. Moose hunting solo is a fool's game, and even with a partner or two it isn't for amateurs. There are good options, such as floating rivers, but whatever recovery methods are available, a great key to moose hunting is under-standing that you can't hunt beyond your ability to get the meat out in a timely fashion.

Guides aren't magicians, by the way — and although they may be young and strong, they also aren't packhorses. A good guide may well tell you that you can't shoot a given moose because you can't get it out — and you'd best listen.

As you've gathered, I'm extremely high on Newfoundland's moose hunting. And yet I'm the only guy I know who needed four Newfoundland moose hunts to take a good eastern moose. I final-ly got a great bull in 2003, but over the course of three hunts in Newfoundland I never shot at a bull moose. Part of it was being picky, part of it was bad weather, and a large part was bad luck. Part, too, was sheer logistics.

On the last day of a Newfie hunt several years ago we went about as far from camp as we ought to go, and then we went a bit farther. We were on a long ridge that dropped away into a river valley. Across the river the ground rose again in a big, brushy ridge. Far up on that sidehill were not one but three very big bull moose. The smallest was a good bull for Newfoundland, and the largest was a good bull for anywhere.

We could probably get across the river, and we could probably reach the moose well before dark. And if we could do that, we could almost certainly get back to camp before the charter plane back to civilization landed in the morning. But there was absolutely no way we could shoot a moose and get it out. So we watched them through my spotting scope for a long, long time. And then we packed up and hunted our way back toward camp.

FOR MILLIONS OF AMERICANS THE WHITETAIL DEER DEFINES THE HUNTING EXPERIENCE... AND A DARNED GOOD DEFINITION HE PROVIDES!

The whitetail deer is more than just another of our North American big-game animals. He's a phenomenon that's at the center of a culture, an industry... almost a religion. Those of you living east of the Great Plains will absolutely understand what I'm talking about. Those of you who live west of the Rockies may not understand this at all. And those of you in the middle may be somewhat divided. But look at it this way: in the West we're blessed with a wide variety of big game. Depending on the area, we have mule deer, blacktails, maybe whitetails, maybe Coues' deer. We have elk and black bear, and permits for moose, goat, sheep, and more. In the East we have a little bit of black bear hunting, very few moose permits... and we have millions of whitetail deer. The whitetail deer is big-game hunting for most hunters in the eastern half of the United States.

This would be important anyway, but it's especially important because hunter densities pretty much follow the population curve. There are more hunters in the East than the West, but I wonder to what extent this is because of the whitetail deer? American hunters have always pursued the game that was most available. In the 1920s and 1930s, when big game was at its lowest ebb, waterfowling was the most popular pursuit among American hunters. Uncontrolled market gunning coupled with the great drought of the Thirties ended the great days of waterfowling, but conditions were changing. FDR's "soil bank" made untold acreage ideal for upland birds, and then there were thousands of acres of small farms that lay fallow during World War II. Millions of G.I.s returning from the war found unprecedented populations of upland birds. The Forties and Fifties were the years of the quail, pheasant, and grouse hunter. But slowly, slowly the whitetail deer was coming back. And suddenly he was there.

Land use changed again, with big, clean farming spelling an end to the great upland bird hunting I knew as a kid. But the whitetail deer didn't care. As late as the 1950s most areas had mere remnant populations. My own home state of Kansas didn't have a modern deer season until 1965. When I was growing up we never saw deer, and even the sight of a track was cause for celebration. Of course we know what Midwest whitetail hunting is like today! I don't know exactly when the whitetail population explosion really kicked off. It varied a little bit with the area, but by the 1960s it was in full swing in the eastern half of the United States. From remnant populations that had retreated into the deepest swamps and forests, the whitetail deer exploded. He proved himself to be incredibly adaptable, and given a little bit of protection he turned out to be best-suited to the edge habitat created by man's agriculture. Thanks to his crafty ways, it turned out that the new legions of whitetail deer required a great deal of hunting to keep their numbers in bounds — and this has translated into unprecedented hunting opportunities.

The whitetail deer is wonderfully democratic. You find him on public land and you find him on private land. Many of the seasons for him seem absurdly long by Western standards, and some of the bag limits seem downright obscene. Alabama, for instance, boasts a "buck a day" limit through a season running three months and more. Some South Carolina counties open in August and close in December — and the tradition there is "no limit on bucks." We in the West, accustomed to much lower wildlife densities, ever-shortening seasons, and one-buck limits, cannot comprehend such bounty, but what we mostly don't understand is that these limits and seasons are set for the most hunter-educated game animals in the world. A few very good hunters with equally good places to hunt take a lot of deer under such rules. But in general the odds still ride with the whitetails!

We have something like 10 million deer hunters in the United States, and of course most of them pursue the whitetail deer — of which there are at least 25 million today. Without a doubt the whitetail deer wouldn't exist in such plenty if not for the conservation efforts of hunters. But I'm not sure we as

I had back-to-back successful Canadian whitetail hunts in 2000 and 2001 — but I earned it; I had made several trips without getting a chance at a mature buck. The Canadian whitetail hunting is wonderful, but not everyone will get a deer.

hunters appreciate the debt we owe to the whitetail. Hunters are a much smaller percentage of the population than we have ever been, but without the whitetail deer we would be a much smaller minority yet. It's the whitetail, and only the whitetail, that has kept hunting strong in Pennsylvania, New York, the Deep South, the Great Lakes region, Texas, and more. Waterfowling, sadly, has become sport for those who can afford duck clubs. Great upland gunning is a thing of the past. But whitetail hunting remains available to all. Unlike waterfowl and upland birds, whitetails thrive in the National Forests, as well as on private land. Hunting opportunity is uneven and varies dramatically, but the key point is that there is opportunity to hunt the whitetail deer available to all. Opening day of deer season remains the major event of the year across a tremendous amount of whitetail range — and I simply can't imagine an end to hunting in areas where the whitetail is king.

This is in stark contrast to California, where I've lived for much of the last 20 years. California was once a great hunting state, and we still have some pretty good deer hunting here and there. But we don't have the whitetail deer. Our hunting opportunity has continued to decline, and many California hunters have given up. As a percentage of population California hunters aren't even worth talking about anymore. In a recent season deer tag returns showed just 30,000-odd deer taken by California hunters, this in one of the largest western states that used to have one of the largest deer herds. We could lose hunting in California and there are few of us left who would care. We don't have the whitetail deer. Ask the million Pennsylvania deer hunters who hit the woods on opening day whether deer hunting is important to them or not!

Any sport that has 10 million active participants is likely to have created a considerable industry, and indeed the whitetail has. There must be at least four dozen "designer" camouflage patterns. There are treestands, ladder stands, self-climbers, tripods, ground blinds by the score. Virtually any centerfire I can think of that's well-suited for whitetail would also be effective for a variety of other big game. But look at the tremendous improvements in shotgun slugs, and in both barrels and special-purpose shotguns designed for slugs in recent years. These may have other uses, but they were designed for the eastern whitetail hunter obligated by local law to use slugs. Even the current spate of in-line muzzleloaders was sparked primarily by whitetail hunters who wanted to take advantage of special muzzleloading seasons. And I'd be willing to bet at least 90 percent of the bowhunting industry revolves around whitetail hunting.

Then there are the high-tech products, those gadgets and gimmicks we all buy so we can be just a little bit more successful: calls, lures, cover scents, decoys, synthetic rattling antlers, you name it. Within reasonable limits, it seems that anything you can think of that just might help bag a whitetail is marketable. And you know what? Most of these things work (at least some of the time)!

As a westerner I grew up hunting with legs and binoculars — in that order. These days I hunt mostly with binoculars and legs — in that order. There are certainly places where you can hunt whitetails this way, but not where the vast majority of our 10 million whitetail hunters hunt them! Whitetail deer aren't easy anywhere, but in the forests and woodlots and edge habitat all across the eastern half of the United States they're quite possibly the most difficult quarry on earth. This is not entirely because the whitetail deer is a magical and super-intelligent creature. He likes to be in heavy cover, and he has keen senses — all of them. But with the heavy hunting pressure common to this region we provide the eastern whitetail with the most advanced education of any game animal on earth. Due to the intensive harvest his numbers require, we make it so that relatively few bucks live to reach full maturity. Those that do are entirely different creatures, and they are indeed almost bulletproof. They become primarily nocturnal and, homebodies that they are, they know every inch and every hideout in their home range. Hunters who consistently take mature whitetails anywhere east of the Great Plains are indeed hunters without parallel... and they need all the help they can get.

As a westerner I was very slow to come to appreciate some of these gimmicks — the scents and lures and calls and whatnot. In fact, I figured it was all bunk and I could hunt whitetails just like everything else. Again, there are places where you can do this... but not where most folks hunt whitetails. The whitetail loves agriculture, and he will almost always come out to feed if there's grain or soybeans or alfalfa or some other treat. But educated whitetails — especially big educated whitetails — are likely to come out only at night. You can go into the thick stuff after them, but nothing is more difficult. Although you will probably hear the occasional snort and see a white flag now and again, sizing up antlers and shooting is even more difficult than just shooting! So eastern hunters — the majority of all whitetail hunters — play the waiting game. And they sweeten the pot with all the guile available to them.

The amazing thing is that all of these high-tech tactics work. It's just that the whitetail is unpredictable enough that none of them work all of the time! Some are very sensitive as to time of season. For instance, a mock scrape requires rutting activity. Antler rattling works very well when it works, but it works best just at the onset of the rut, and even then there must generally be some competition among the bucks for available does. Decoys are also uneven, but when they work they're awesome. Do I really believe a cover scent can fool a whitetail? Not for long, but sometimes long enough to offer a shot! I find calling extremely effective, and not especially sensitive as to time of season, but it won't work all of the time, and you'll usually never know why. But all of these things and more can work — and depending on the time of season the serious whitetail hunter uses all of them. Here are a few quick examples. I've done a lot of whitetail hunting in Texas, and of course I've always tried to time the rut exactly, but timing the rut is not a game for nonresidents. No matter how hard you try, invariably you'll be a few days off one way or the other. Texas is the center of horn-rattling, although it can work anywhere. But I had rattled my heart out on a bunch of good ranches, and I was getting very skeptical. John Wooters himself rattled in the first buck I ever saw come to the "horns," and it was just like you read about. He was a pretty fair buck and I could have shot him, but I was mostly fascinated by the aggressive behavior he showed as he strode into the clearing and started thrashing a mesquite. Since then I've seen it work a few times, never consistently. The best rattling day I ever had was with Texan Charley White; he rattled up six bucks one afternoon from one stand. You bet it can work – but not always.

A few years ago I was hunting the low country of South Carolina. It was October, fairly early, but there was some pre-rut activity going on. I was sitting in a treestand overlooking a food plot, and there was an active scrape line going off to my left. In spite of a perfect setup, there was absolutely nothing happening,

TOP: Canadian bucks are huge-bodied and their antler potential is unlimited, but deer densities are low. This is a good, mature buck carrying just over 150 inches of antler by B&C measurements. If you pass a buck like this you may not see a better one.
BOTTOM: Texas is the center of antler-rattling for whitetails. The method will actually work anywhere under the right conditions — but it doesn't work all the time anywhere. Nor does anything else.

but it was a very hot, muggy, and still morning and I wasn't too surprised. About nine o'clock, when I was ready to die from boredom, I pulled out a grunt tube and blew a soft series. Using any technique when you're bored and hopeless is dangerous, because you're almost sure to overdo it. So I looked at my watch and made sure 20 minutes passed before I blew the call again — sparingly. Right after the third series a nice eight-pointer swaggered in from my left, looking for the intruder. He was 30 feet from my tree when I shot him.

Another time, in Alabama, I set up on the edge of some cover overlooking a little plowed field, a likely enough place for a buck to cross based on the topography. My host and friend, Gene Dismukes, had given me some of his "Diz's" deer lure and insisted I try it. So, expecting nothing, I poured some of it onto the ground about 50 yards in front of the stand. I think it was about eight o'clock when a nice little buck came trotting across the field. There was all the time in the world, so I let him come. He hit the scent stream from that lure, slammed on the brakes, turned into it, and had his head down and was pawing at the stuff when I shot him. Mind you, it isn't always that easy. In fact, it almost never is. But there's nothing wrong with having a full repertoire of tricks and tactics at your disposal. With the whitetail you usually need them!

You also need a good place to hunt them, especially if you're interested in big, fully mature bucks. A far better whitetail hunter than I am said it better than I ever could: How you hunt whitetails probably isn't nearly as important as where you hunt them! You can study the records book as well as I can, and if you do so you'll quickly discover that there are jut a few notice-able hot spots. Wisconsin and Minnesota have always produced large numbers of big bucks. Western Canada is very good, and these days the Midwest is truly astonishing — Iowa, Ohio, Illinois, Kansas, and northern Missouri.

It's also worth noting that a big buck can turn up darn near anywhere in their vast domain. To a degree this depends on your concept of a big buck. If you mean a buck scoring 200 typical points there are very few places where you have even a ghost of a chance. If you mean a buck scoring the All-time minimum for typical whitetails of 170 points there are a few more spots. If you mean 160 points, the minimum for the three-year books, then there are quite a lot of places. And if you mean a nice, heavy-antlered buck of 4-1/2 years or more, then such a buck can turn up anywhere.

We hunters, being human, tend to believe the grass is always greener somewhere else. Usually it isn't, and it definitely isn't with the whitetail. Put this in the bank: The best place to hunt whitetail deer is in your backyard. This is assuming first that you have whitetail deer where you live, and that you can find a place to hunt where you don't have to fight the crowds. Given these two conditions, the best chances for trophy whitetail are close to home. You can scout the off-season and find out what's really there, and you can find out where the deer are living and exactly what they're feeding on at different times of the year. And you can be patient and bide your time. In most states you can hunt the bow season and the blackpowder season and finally the rifle season. You can wait for the peak of the rut to go into your secret spots, and if the wind is unfavorable you can sit out for a day or a weekend. When you travel far from home you can do none of these things. Whitetail hunting, at its best, is an insider's game — and most of the really great whitetail deer have been taken by residents hunting close to home.

These are the facts, but human nature being as it is, sooner or later most serious whitetail hunters are likely to convince themselves that the buck of their dreams lies in some distant state or province. And some of us that covet a big whitetail don't live in whitetail country, so we have little choice but to venture afield. The search will probably not be easy, and the record books are somewhat misleading. There are quite a few areas that produce good numbers of big whitetails... but few of them are user-friendly for outsiders. Research, for instance, points to Wisconsin and Minnesota as two likely spots. Both of these areas, however, have short, intensive seasons and virtually no outfitting industry.

The farmland of western Iowa and southern Illinois is fabulous, and there are a few outfitters springing up in these prime areas. But you'll probably have to hunt with shotguns, muzzleloaders, or archery tackle. That isn't such a bad deal, but it does substantially decrease the odds on the typically short hunt a nonresident is relegated to. Kansas is fabulous... sort of. At long last my home state is offering a few nonresident tags, and I can go home to hunt deer again. But there are few tags in that wonderfully vulnerable river bottom country out west. The areas that are open are good, but not materially better than the woodlot country elsewhere in the Midwest.

Then there's Canada, legendary home to monster whitetails. They're there, all right. Saskatchewan, Alberta, Manitoba, eastern B.C. — all places where you can find the whitetail of a lifetime. But you should have a clear understanding of the odds going in. Very few of even the best outfitters reach 50 percent success, especially when you're talking about mature bucks. If you're talking record-class bucks the percentage is much, much lower. The hunting up there is very weather-sensitive, and the actual deer densities are very low... as low as one deer per square mile in some of the best trophy country.

If it sounds like I'm down on Canadian whitetail hunting, I'm not. The monsters are there, and well they should be. Three-hundred-pound whitetail can grow bigger antlers than deer half this size! But it's realistic to understand that a Canadian hunt is a post-graduate whitetail hunt; it's going for the long ball, and I believe that's what you should go for. In three trips to Alberta I never fired a shot, although I turned down some bucks I wouldn't turn down anyplace else. In 2000 and 2001, I hunted in Saskatchewan and pretty much reversed this trend. Both times I got very nice, heavy horned, grown-up bucks, both scoring in the mid-150s. Yes, I had in mind something a bit larger, but both these bucks were taken late in the hunt, and both were the largest deer I saw. There are very good bucks in Canada, but if you turn down a mature, heavy-antlered, big-bodied buck scoring maybe 150 or better there is a very good chance you have just turned down the best buck you will see.

Without a doubt Texas is the most user-friendly state for nonresidents to hunt whitetails. The deer there are an industry, and whitetails are managed wonderfully on good private ranches. Which is not to say the whole state is trophy country — it depends on what you're looking for. Throughout the Hill Country and Edwards Plateau you can enjoy a fun hunt where you'll see lots and lots of deer. You probably won't see any monsters, but not everybody is looking for a monster. Down along the Gulf Coast you'll see a little better class of deer — still a fun hunt in

TOP: The Great Plains doesn't look much like whitetail country, especially if you're used to the eastern woods, but the whitetails don't seem to agree. They're increasing by leaps and bounds all along the eastern front of the Rockies, making this whole region one of the best hot spots in the country.
BOTTOM: A really nice plains whitetail, taken in badland country in western Kansas. I like hunting plains whitetails because, in the relatively open country, you can glass, salk, and still-hunt effectively.

much different country, and real big ones are rare. But you can see a lot of deer and enjoy a fine hunt. Or you can go to the famed Brush Country of South Texas and get serious. You'll undoubtedly see a lot fewer deer, but the upper end gets a good deal larger. My own best-ever whitetail came from Texas, but keep in mind that genuine monsters aren't lurking behind every bush. In the real trophy country you're out of the sure-thing business, and the best hunting is very rut-sensitive. But if you do good research in both picking a time and an outfitter the chances for a very nice buck are pretty good. The real draw-back to Texas hunting is that the best trophy ranches are just plain expensive, definitely not for everybody.

It's impossible to talk about the whole world of whitetail hunting in one article — it's just too big. But a wonderful and often-over-looked region is the entire Great Plains, east of the Rockies and west of the corn belt. There aren't many non-resident tags in western Kansas, but there are a few. I drew there in '99, and despite unseasonably hot weather I took a wonderful "mid-160s" sort of a buck. You can get also get tags in western Oklahoma, eastern Colorado, western Nebraska, eastern Wyoming, the western Dakotas, and east-ern Montana. All of these are good, and there's a good outfit-ting industry in Colorado, Wyoming, and Montana. Most of the whitetails are on private land, but provided you're willing to do some research there's also good opportunity for do-it-yourself hunting.

The upper end of the bucks in this region is generally not as big as the best Canadian bucks, but it's pretty darned good. Deer densities are generally not high, but they tend to follow the river bottoms. Mind you, that isn't exactly the same as liv-ing in the river bottoms — many of the best bucks have figured out that's where hunters look for them, and these days we often find big whitetails out in the sagebrush. The good thing about this region is that it's both huntable and very lightly hunted. In some areas you can glass for whitetails just like pronghorn and mulies, and in other areas you can stand-hunt along the river bottoms, but it's an awful lot of fun.

A few years ago, Kevin Howard and I watched through binoculars as *Deer & Deer Hunting's* Pat Durkin and outfitter Tom Tietz stalked a wonderful whitetail on some open sage-brush ridges — darn near a spectator sport. We got that one. Two days earlier we bedded a buck up in some high rimrock, and when we got there we just couldn't find him. He came out of some rocks right under my feet, but it wasn't my shot. He hung in midair right next to me, a big, beautiful 10-pointer, and then he was off like a broken-field runner, speeded along the way by some parting salutes.

The western Great Plains has become my favorite area to hunt whitetails. I've hunted with and guided for Tom Tietz in Colorado, and I've hunted with Mike Watkin's Trophies Plus outfit in northeastern Wyoming, southeastern Montana, and adjacent South Dakota. I also hunted in western Nebraska and found wonderfully unsophisticated river bottom bucks. All of this region is excellent, so there is tremendous opportunity, but keep in mind that almost nowhere are the licenses easy to come by. Part of the reason it's good is because the hunting is limited, so you have to do your homework and plan ahead. Sometimes way ahead — it takes a couple of years to get a good eastern Colorado tag, courtesy of the preference point system. I think it's worth the wait.

The truth, however, is that hunting whitetails on the Great Plains, or on a good ranch in Texas, or even hunting those scarce monsters in Canada, is simply not the same as hunting those hard-hunted Eastern whitetails. In fact, it's hardly like hunting the same animal. You need to hunt those hunter-educated, virtually unkillable bucks in the Eastern forests and swamps to really appreciate these places. Which is no doubt why so many hunters from great Eastern whitetail country travel West every year. I'm still not sure the grass is really greener, but I don't really blame them!

CHAPTER FOURTEEN ▪ COUGAR
The Great North American Cat

THE COUGAR IS AMERICA'S MOST MISUNDERSTOOD BIG GAME ANIMAL.

Just the other day I read that a Colorado mountain lion killed one unfortunate youngster and badly mauled another. I haven't been keeping score, but it's no secret that such tragedies have become increasingly common in recent years. In fact, there's no measurement for the percentage of increase. During the first few hundred years of European occupation of North America there were virtually no authenticated cases of a cougar attacking a human. Rumors, yes. Legends, for sure. Campfire tales, by the dozen, but almost no hard evidence. During the last several years there have been a number of well-documented and highly publicized attacks, including several human fatalities. That's an important qualifier, for a cougar attack on a person almost always results in the death of the cougar. Sometimes even the offending one.

In great contradiction to this, I still see cougars as a common figure in animal rights and antihunting propaganda. This is because they are beautiful creatures and, if photographed in the proper light, appear anthropomorphically cute and cuddly. I don't have a problem with that, but I'm getting awfully tired of hearing them described as "endangered."

So what's the truth about the cougar? Is he some kind of a man-eating monster, or a teddy bear in feline clothing? Is he endangered? Of course he's none of these things. The cougar, or mountain lion, panther, painter, catamount, or whatever you choose to call him, is just what he is: A big, beautiful cat that is exceptionally shy and secretive, a bit of a loner, and also one of the most efficient predators in the world.

The mountain lion has absolutely no problem killing big deer twice his size, and is known to kill elk five times his size. These are his natural prey, and his normal diet is generally considered to approach a deer per week. However, like all cats he can be a bit on the lazy side. Especially when game is short he may develop a taste for veal, and he often shows a strong preference for mutton or horse foals. The ease with which he pulls down quadrupeds much larger than he is astonishing. However, no one can seriously suggest that the cougar is dangerous game. If he had the disposition of the leopard he would be, but he does not.

The leopard is nocturnal and shy, but he can be very aggressive. Although the leopard is a much smaller cat than the mountain lion, there are numerous case histories of man-eating leopards in both India and Africa. The American mountain lion has certainly killed humans in recent years, and has certainly eaten its prey, but we have no history of repeated maneaters like the Rudraprayag leopard that Colonel Jim Corbett killed... after it had claimed dozens of victims. Our mountain lion has the equipment and the know how to use it, but historically has kept people off the menu.

I think the difference today comes from three primary causes. First, and perhaps most importantly, urban sprawl is putting more people into inadvertent contact with mountain lions. As people move into the scenic suburbs in increasing numbers they are more likely to encounter cougars. Most times people will be totally unaware that a cougar is anywhere near, but once in a while accidents happen. Some of the recent tragedies have appeared to be just that: accidents of mistaken identification. A cougar lies in wait along a game trail, perhaps a trail that has yielded dinner in the past. A jogger comes by, and the cat's natural instincts come into play before its brain becomes engaged. This doesn't make it any less tragic, but it falls short of being diabolical.

In some areas an underlying reason for increased attacks on humans, as well as livestock depredation, is an unnatural imbalance between predator and prey. Although there have been recent man/cougar incidents in Idaho, Montana, and most other western states, both Colorado and California seem to have hosted an unnatural share. But look at the situation. Both states have a lot of ideal cougar habitat, and both have always been home to healthy populations of the great cats. Colorado has sharply limited cougar hunting these days, and California

I took this very good tom cougar in southwestern Arizona. Although I used a handgun, choice of equipment doesn't add to the challenge in cougar hunting. The hunt is very much the chase, not the kill.

has had no sport hunting for a quartercentury. Cougars are exceptionally difficult to count, but both states probably have an all-time high population. Both states are classic examples of urban sprawl, with people buying "ranchettes" and moving into hills and mountains in large numbers. The stage is thus set for unprecedented potential for man/cougar contact.

Now add in near all-time lows in deer populations in both states. In Colorado the causes have been loss of habitat, especially winter range, coupled with tough winters; and a tremendous explosion in elk, which are indeed natural prey for cougars, but not the preferred diet. In California the causes are drought, loss of habitat, and the cougars themselves. When the mountain lion was protected back in 1971 it was estimated that California might hold 2,000 cougars. Today the estimates range from 5,000 to 7,000 and beyond, and many experts feel these are conservative figures.

Given the chance, a cougar might kill and eat a deer per week. Certainly 40 a year is not an exaggerated figure. In a recent season, California deer tag returns indicated that the sportsmen's harvest was a mere 30,000 deer. Deer tag returns are not exactly mandatory, so the legal harvest is probably a bit higher, but not by much. In the same year, some 70,000 deer were reported killed on roads and highways. Depending on how conservative you want to be, California's cougars killed from 200,000 to 350,000 deer that year... if they could find them. The Golden State deer herd was never estimated at much more than 750,000, so it doesn't take a mathematician to figure out that the cougars' harvest is not sustainable.

The Central Coast, where I live, is a classic example. Just 15 years ago it was a deer factory; it wasn't uncommon to see more than a hundred in a single field. Then came the drought. Then came the wine industry, with high fences and easy-to-obtain depredation permits to protect the invaluable grapes. Then came the Conservation Reserve Program (CRP), which has done wonders for birds, but has taken a lot of row crop acreage that the deer loved out of production. The cougars have always been there, and they still are, but deer are downright scarce. Cougar depredation is at an all-time high, and so are man/cougar encounters. Sad to say, the stage is set for more tragedies.

A third factor is the fact that there is little cougar hunting being done today, even in the prime western states and Canadian provinces. The most reviled group in our sporting fraternity is the houndsman, a great and unfortunate shift from our heritage. Hunting with hounds was the preferred hunting method of no less than Daniel Boone and Davy Crockett, and it is virtually the only reliable way to hunt the elusive cougar. It was also a favorite hunting method of B&C's founder Theodore Roosevelt, who, while he was President, took a fine cougar that is still listed in the all-time *Records of North American Big Game*. Things are different today. Much of society, including many hunters, seem to have decided that hound hunting is unsporting. Hound hunting has been legislated out of existence in several states. Even where legal, many houndsmen have given up under the pressure and the grim economic reality of the impracticality of keeping a pack of hounds for ever-shortening seasons.

There isn't a lot of cougar hunting going on, and one could theorize that the cougars, now completely unbothered, have lost their centuries-old respect for man. Certainly there are a lot more near misses than ever before, with reports of people being stalked by cougars and finding them in their backyards relatively commonplace.

In years gone by an experienced hunter could spend a lifetime in cougar country and never see more than tracks and scat. These days, in much of the west, daylight sightings are no longer unusual. In light of all this, continued propaganda about the "endangered" cougar is just plain ridiculous. Although he is still extremely uncommon in the eastern half of the country, he has basically recaptured most of his former range, and certainly exists in huntable numbers from the western Great Plains to the Pacific. The small Florida cougar is indeed seriously threatened, but as a species *Felis concolor* is quite secure. More secure, perhaps, than much of his prey and those who hunt him!

Mind you, none of this is to say that the cougar should be considered "dangerous game." Certainly he should not be. Many of the recent tragedies have involved children, youngsters, and women, almost never a full-grown man. And never an armed hunter who was pursuing a cougar. Although we call him "mountain lion" and sometimes just "lion," our cougar is not a lion, nor a tiger, nor a leopard. He is an exceptionally efficient hunter and sometimes, like the cat he is, he will kill to excess in a flock of sheep or a winter yard of deer. But except in those flashing moments when he works for his dinner, he is not ferocious by nature. He is reticent and shy, and extremely difficult to see, especially on purpose. I know a very few dedicated predator callers who have called in mountain lions. More often than not this is a natural accident that results from countless hours of blowing a predator call in lion country. In other words, a mountain lion was called in while calling bobcats or coyotes. I also know some very dedicated predator callers who have spent countless hours trying to call in a mountain lion, without success. It isn't that they won't come to a call. They will. Rather, it's that they're generally solitary hunters who range widely over big country. You can't call in anything unless it hears you calling, and it takes a huge measure of luck to be in exactly the right place at the right time for a cat to hear you... and be in the mood to respond.

I also know several people who have simply blundered into cougars while hunting something else and have wound up with a mountain lion rug for their trouble. It happens, but it's a lot like buying a lottery ticket. You have to have a lottery ticket to win, and you have to have a cougar license to play. The odds are much the same. I've actually bumped into cougars in the wild three times, which is quite a lot, but never with a license nor an open season. In good country there's nothing wrong with buying a tag, especially since there are more cougars than ever before. But don't count on it...

Over the years I have read and heard told that a good man on snowshoes could walk down a cougar in tracking snow. I don't know any man who has actually done it — but I know one woman who has. Debra Bradbury of Glenrock, Wyoming, publisher of *Blackpowder Hunter*, a Professional Member of Boone and Crockett and former editor of *Fair Chase*, and one of the best rifle shots I know, got it in her mind that she wanted to take a cougar without using dogs. She lives in good cougar country that offers several months of snow, so she had that advantage. She is also an ardent coyote hunter, so she knows her country and, during the winter, is out and about a great deal.

Debra searched for fresh cougar tracks for three winters, and several times found tracks fresh enough to follow. A couple she jumped without seeing, some just plain outran her, and other times darkness ended the chase. Then, early one morning, she found the fresh tracks of a good cat. She followed throughout the morning, sometimes losing the tracks where the wind had swept the hills clean, then casting ahead to find them again. The track wound endlessly through sage-brush hills and timbered pockets, and it seemed certain this was another wild goose chase.

In the afternoon she found a fresh kill... and fresher tracks. She pressed on, and after an hour or so she saw a tawny form on the far side of a clearing, just about to drift into a stand of evergreens. One shot from her .270, and she accomplished a hunting feat that I had considered to be just a legend.

Most of us who choose to hunt cougars do so with the aid of hounds! Regardless of the bad press hound hunting has received, this is the only reasonably reliable way to hunt a cougar. It is not a sure thing. Even in good country the big cats are thinly scattered and range widely, and it can take many days to find a track. Sometimes you don't find one! Once you find a track and turn loose the pack, it is still not a sure thing. Like most cats, cougars are shortwinded and the average chase is not long. However, sometimes the chase outdistances the hunter. Sometimes the hunters can't keep up. And sometimes the cat loses the dogs in the rugged country they call home. No two chases are alike, and you never know what might happen when you turn loose the dogs. However, cougar hunting with hounds is generally successful, more so than hound hunting for bears because of the cougar's short wind and a more natural tendency to take to a tree.

There are no other truly viable ways to take a cougar, so there are no exact parallels with bear hunting. However, as is the case with hunting black bears with dogs, hound hunting is also extremely selective. Very few people have seen enough cougars to know whether a cat that is accidentally encountered or comes to a varmint call is mature or not. Plus, given an opportunity, a tag, and an open season, fewer would stop to check. With hound hunting there is no reason for a mistake; you have seen the tracks and you will see the treed cougar at close range. If he isn't what you want you can walk away.

Two other things about hound hunting are widely misunderstood. First, it's an extremely physical hunt. You simply have to keep within earshot of the hounds, and that can mean a mad scramble through extremely tough real estate or slogging through deep snow with or without snowshoes, depending on whether or not you have them. The other thing about cougar hunting that those who haven't tried it don't understand is that it's extremely exciting. Listening to the chase, scrambling from ridge to ridge, and then closing in on the cacophony of hounds around the tree is a thrilling experience. What's different about cougar hunting from most other hunting experiences is that the chase is everything, and the shot is anticlimactic.

Most of the time it is an extremely simple thing to shoot a treed cougar. As in all hunting, the shot must be placed well, but in cougar hunting this is especially important lest the hounds be endangered by a wounded cat. However, the shot will not be difficult. No special equipment is required, nor is a great deal of power needed. Cougars are not particularly hardy, and the shot is close enough that precise placement should be assured. Some cougar hunters use guns as light as .22 magnums, and the old .25-20 and .32-20 are favorites among houndsmen. Traditional centerfires in the deer class are not needed and are overly destructive especially at the very short ranges common with hound hunting.

Many use handguns and archery tackle to add to the challenge. Such tackle is certainly effective enough, but this misses the point. It isn't the shot that matters; it's getting to the tree and being part of the chase. In this regard, the unfortunate part about cougar hunting is that the real enjoyment of the hunt belongs to the houndsman alone. He has raised and trained his dogs and knows the sound each one makes. He can stand on a rocky point and listen to a chase on the next mountain and know which dog is in the lead. He will know when the trail is cold and when it gets hot, he will know when the cougar is jumped, and he will know exactly and precisely when it trees. You or I who are not houndsmen will know none of these things, and our experience of a cougar hunt is much the poorer for the lack.

I am not a houndsman, and I much prefer hunting in which I can fully participate. I can appreciate an exciting chase, and I'm enough of a runner to enjoy the hard scramble in getting to the tree, but I am also a rifleman, and the kind of shooting required doesn't appeal to me. So nearly 20 years have passed since my last cougar hunt. In that I was exceptionally fortunate; I hunted with Arizona legends Warner

TOP: Cougars are highly efficient hunters and have the equipment to be dangerous. However, they do not have the disposition of other great cats and it takes unusual circumstances for them to be a menace to man.
BOTTOM: In hound hunting, there is definitely danger... but it's mostly to the hounds. Warner Glenn is doing some quick surgery on a courageous dog that got too close.

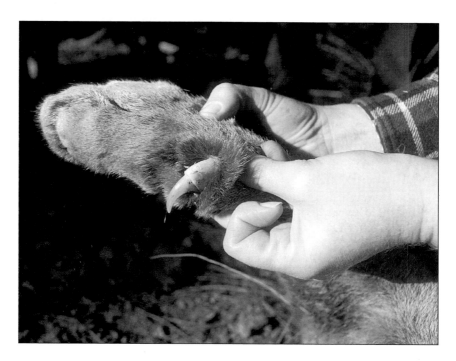

Glenn and his father, the late Marvin Glenn. Gentlemen both, soft-spoken and men of few words, they nevertheless were anxious to share their mountains and explain the intricacies of the chase as it unfolded. I pity the cougar hunter who is simply taken to tree and sent home with his cougar by a taciturn houndsman and I fear that is often the case.

With the Glenn's we combed the rugged Chiricahua and Dragoon Mountains for a few days looking for tracks. We explored Indian caves, treed the first coati mundi I'd ever seen, and followed a couple of tracks that proved too cold in the dry Arizona air. And then a neighbor called and reported that he had found a fresh javelina kill. We trailered the riding mules and dogs to the spot, found a day-old kill, and shortly we were on a hell-for-leather chase through rugged rimrock country. The cat, a very big tom, treed in a huge Ponderosa pine. I still have the rug and the skull, boiled out for me by Margaret Glenn in her pressure cooker. They are prized trophies, but what I remember most is sharing the hunt with such fine people.

It was an enjoyable hunt, but for the reasons stated it is not one that I have an overwhelming desire to repeat. Which is a good thing. Although the cougar remains legal game in most western states, about a decade ago, after years of a moratorium on cougar hunting, California changed the cougar to a non-game animal, in effect a sacred cow. The game department cannot manage them and sportsmen cannot hunt them; all we can do is feed our dwindling deer herd to their increasing numbers. And a California resident, although a citizen of the United States in most contexts of the Constitution, cannot lawfully bring a legally-taken sporthunted cougar into the state of California. Since that's where I live, and since I lack the wherewithal to challenge such an outrageous law, chances are I will hunt no more cougars in my lifetime.

On the other hand, I am an absolute proponent of cougar hunting and hound hunting. Cougar hunting because, like all wildlife resources, the great cats need to be managed. Allowing Mother Nature to maintain her own balance is a wonderful idea in a perfect world, but the world hasn't been perfect since Man started leaving lots of footprints. In a natural state the great predators exhaust their prey and move on, but in Man's world there isn't always anyplace left for them to go. So first they run out of prey, and then they starve or, driven by hunger, they commit what we consider crimes and are executed for them.

It's a comforting thing to know that the wild places of the West are still cougar country, but I don't want them in the backyard with my kids... and I'd like to have some deer around as well. So I'm all for managing prey and predator species alike, making sure that there are deer to watch and occasionally hunt... and enough cougars so that I can see their tracks once in a while, and just maybe catch a glimpse of one every few years.

I'm all for hound hunting, too. Not because I'm a houndsman, but because, over the last two centuries, it remains the only reliable way to hunt cougars, and is an equally effective and selective way to hunt bears. And not just for that reason alone. It's a traditional and time-honored sport still pursued by a dying breed of individualists... and they are hunters, just like all the rest of us who are not houndsmen. In the states where hound hunting has been outlawed the vote would have been different had sportsmen stuck together. Instead many of us, perhaps well-intentioned, but extremely shortsighted, turned on our own. We as hunters are not only individualists, but we're often narrow-minded elitists quick to scorn hunting methods we don't understand. It makes me tired to hear talk that hound hunting isn't "fair chase," or that baiting for bears isn't "fair chase." Good Lord, more than a dozen states allow baiting for deer, and as far as I know nobody thinks hunting quail over dogs is unsporting.

If you don't like it, don't do it, but keep in mind that local hunting techniques are usually developed from hunting conditions. Hunters learned centuries ago that gamebirds were much easier to locate with the help of a canine nose. Similarly, that deer were drawn to apples and corn. Most of the states that allow baiting have heavy cover, where spot-and-stalk techniques are not only difficult, but unproductive. I suspect baiting remains legal in many areas not only because it's so traditional that few think twice about it, but also because it helps keep the harvest of the prolific whitetail at management goals. Bear are traditionally baited or run with hounds in areas where the cover is so thick that other methods just won't work. And with cougars it's the only game in town. Well, not exactly. Debra Bradbury proved there are other means. Her three-year quest, an admirable exercise in determination and woodcraft, stands as one of the most singular hunting feats I'm aware of, and certainly redefines fair chase... but it is not an effective management tool. Hound hunting is.

CHAPTER FIFTEEN - BLACKTAIL
More Than Just Small Mule Deer

THE DEER OF THE PACIFIC NORTHWEST AREN'T JUST MINIATURE MULIES THEY'RE ALTOGETHER DIFFERENT AND DELIGHTFUL!

The serious hunters who live in blacktail country love their local deer just as much as American deer hunters everywhere love their homegrown deer. In fact, deer hunters in western Oregon and Washington and northwestern California are just as avid as Pennsylvania whitetail hunters, Colorado mule deer hunters, and Arizona Coues' deer hunters. You just don't hear too much about them because, for some reason, very few outsiders give a darn about blacktail deer. Except for the local hunters who pursue them (and religiously guard their secret hot-spots), the blacktail deer is far and away the least known, the least publicized, and the least pursued deer by "outsiders."

I'm not altogether sure why this should be, but I suspect it stems from a number of factors. For one thing, to be honest, blacktail hunting is very much an insider's game. The public hunting areas that are any good for Columbia blacktail (and some are very good indeed) tend to be either very high, very thick, or both. Access to private land is difficult, and there is just a tiny handful of outfitters who specialize in blacktail deer. Perhaps there would be more, but deer hunters from all over the country aren't beating down outfitters' doors looking for good blacktails the way they are for good whitetail, mule deer, and Coues' deer hunting.

The situation is just the reverse for Sitka blacktail hunting. There is literally unlimited public land available, and virtually every bear outfitter on Kodiak and the other Sitka hot-spots would dearly love to extend his season by taking deer hunters... but they have trouble finding hunters and a harder time charging enough to cover their very considerable outfitting costs.

for plains whitetails as well. But there's a difference. Blacktails are more cover-loving than mule deer, and they're also more habitual. You can glass for them, and you should if there are openings to glass, but it's tighter glassing than is normally done for mule deer, and you're much more likely to spot the same bucks in the same places. In most areas blacktails hang in the thick stuff as much as they can, and they often follow known trails. In fact, one of the most interesting things about black-tails is that they're a lot like whitetails. Given time and a clear playing field you can pattern them. You can also rattle them up and call them. None of these methods work all the time... but, then, they don't work all the time on whitetails, either.

I attribute this to the fact that blacktails live in heavier cover than mule deer, and have adapted accordingly. They rely on their ears and sense of smell more than their eyes, which is typically the mule deer's first line of defense. In the thick forests of western Oregon and Washington and coastal British Columbia, serious blacktail hunters hunt their deer just like eastern sportsmen hunt their whitetails: they sit on trails, and they rattle, and they call. Mule deer can be hunted by these techniques, but blacktails typically respond to calling and rat-tling far more readily than mule deer... and, during the rut, they also respond extremely well to decoys!

Although they're clearly a mule deer subspecies, they've simply adapted to closer cover. They are also significantly different in appearance than mule deer. They're smaller, yes, and in both body and antler, but the blacktail is more than just a small mule deer. The black upper surface of the tail is distinctive, but so are other characteristics. The ears are much smaller and more rounded — not so small or round as the whitetail's, but not nearly so exaggerated as a mule deer. The face is much smaller and more pixie-like, and there are usually attractive black highlights on the nose and forehead. Capes vary tremendously, but typically the blacktail has a prominent white throat patch, much more similar to a whitetail's than the more subdued throat patch of a mulie. Many blacktails, though not all, display a particularly attractive double throat patch.

The antlers are definitely smaller than a mule deer's; there's a difference of 55 Boone and Crockett points — 55 inches of antler — between the minimum score for Columbia black-tail and the minimum score for mule deer. While mule deer hunters dream of 30-inch spreads, a blacktail with a 20-inch spread is a darned good deer. These much smaller antlers, however, are perfectly in scale with the blacktail's ear width and facial dimensions. A good blacktail with a brilliant cape is one of the most beautiful of our deer, and will stand out in any trophy collection.

There is much confusion regarding exactly what comprises a good blacktail. Everybody wants a four-by-four with eye guards, and provided such a buck is fully mature and carries a bit of mass that is a great blacktail. Non-typicals do occur, but are very rare — much more rare than is the case with mule deer. In truth, except in a very few carefully-managed areas with very good genetics, typical four-by-fours are also quite rare. Many very good blacktails never get beyond three fighting tines per side. As is true with mule deer, strong brow points are extremely rare, and many big blacktails lack brow points altogether. With blacktails it's probably better to look for mass, spread, and point length before you count tines. Three-by-three blacktails are well-represented in the All-time records book, even after the minimum score was raised. I've also seen (and shot) big forkie blacktails that are in all ways representative and respectable trophies.

It isn't essential that one be a trophy hunter to pursue blacktails. They're a challenging and fascinating animal, and, like all of our deer, their venison is tasty. (Personally, I rate them better than mule deer, though grain-fed whitetail is hard to beat!) Their habitat is beautiful, although it varies too much to characterize. In the southern and eastern portions of their ranges you can hunt them in rolling oak grasslands, interspersed with hillsides of manzanita and chaparral and cut by canyons filled with poison oak.Or you can hunt them in groves of giant redwoods. Or you can hunt them in the high Alpine at the top of the Cascades. Or in the lush rain forests of the Pacific Northwest. Each of these habitats are unique and beautiful. However, you should keep in mind two things. First, the thicker the vegetation the more difficult the hunting. Second, antler growth is generally reduced in the very thick forests of northwestern Oregon, western Washington, and coastal British Columbia. This is almost certainly due to limited antler-producing nutrients in the conifer forests, and is probably the reason why blacktails from the more mixed vegetation of northern California and southwestern Oregon dominate the records-book listings.

Again, you don't have to be a trophy hunter to enjoy blacktail hunting. But if you are there is a caution that must be applied to blacktails that doesn't exist with our other deer. The range of the Columbia blacktail is not small. For records-keeping purposes it stretches north along the West Coast from south of San Francisco all the way to northern British Columbia. Unfortunately, whenever records-keepers are obligated to define boundaries between subspecies the lines must be drawn somewhere, and this is exceedingly difficult with blacktail deer.

In the north it's virtually impossible to say exactly where *columbianus* really becomes *sitkensis*, but at least both are blacktails. By the time you get to Alaska's offshore islands where most of the hunting is conducted the differences are quite clear. The rub comes in the broad intergrade areas to the south and east, where blacktails bump against California and Rocky Mountain mule deer. My first experience with "blacktails" was on the western slopes of Mount Lassen. That was a great deer herd 20 years ago. One of our big migratory herds that, in the fall, could be seen streaming down out of the high country to summer pasture by the thousand. There are still good deer there, but that herd crashed due to overpopulation and now, with the abundance of predators, probably will never fully recover. These deer are small-bodied, small-eared, typically antlered, and black-tailed, but they fall outside the official blacktail boundary.

I live in central California, as much as a hundred miles south of the "true blacktail line." Although many of the local hunters call our deer "blacktails," it's quite difficult to say exactly what they are. Technically I suppose they're a mix of blacktail and California mule deer. The deer on some of the ranches I hunt show pure blacktail tendencies. You can measure the tarsal glands, and they're correct for blacktailed deer. The tails are pure black on the upper surface, and the ears are small. You can't put much stock in the antlers, because our deer have small, almost stunted antlers — probably due to the long, hot, dry summers. The local deer in other areas — some of which are farther north — show mixed tails and ears that are clearly too big.

In my more argumentative days I corresponded with B&C's stalwart, the late Phil Wright, about trying to redefine the black-

TOP: Classic blacktail country in northern California. Country like this allows glassing, and also has better and more varied food sources than the true forest farther north — two reasons why California and southern Oregon dominate the records for blacktails. BOTTOM: This is Rattler, a very old buck that was massive in both antler and body. He was at least 9-1/2 years old when taken, and had carried much better antlers in his prime.

tail line, but the problem is that there are indeed very large intergrade areas. Mostly this is harmless; it doesn't matter to me if my local "almost blacktails" are called blacktails — especially since it's very unlikely for one to meet the records-book minimum. It probably does matter with herds like that Mount Lassen herd, which are as pure blacktail as you can get, but which just might interbreed with mule deer up in the high country, so have to be classified as mule deer. This is unfortunate, but it really doesn't matter as long as you know.

Unfortunately, the blacktail line isn't able to follow state boundaries or major rivers. If you care about hunting a genuine "B&C" blacktail you have to do your homework. If you don't, someone else may do it for you. In the years when I hunted that Mount Lassen herd I knew they were outside the official line, and I didn't care. But the first time I hunted in Oregon, having booked a "blacktail hunt" with my outfitter, I found myself glassing from a high ridge from which I could look west across Interstate 5. I-5 happens to be the demarcation line between blacktails and mule deer in that particular area, and I was on the wrong side. I wasn't pleased.

On both the south and east sides of the B&C blacktail range there continue to be ranchers and outfitters marketing transition deer as "blacktails." They're probably mostly blacktail, and the hunting isn't necessarily different, but if it's important to you to hunt the "real McCoy," then you'd better check a map.

To me, the beauty of the deer and the country they live in give plenty of reason to hunt blacktails. But there's a bonus: Right now the blacktailed deer offer the greatest trophy opportunity of any of our North American deer. This is certainly not universal across their range; big antlers come hard in the big northwestern forests, and it gets harder the farther north you go. However, on well-managed private lands in the mixed cover of northern California and southwestern Oregon; and in limited entry public land units in both states the opportunity to take a real trophy far exceeds the normal odds with our other deer.

As an example, my buddy Jim Schaafsma is a decade into a management program on a ranch in ideal blacktail habitat. Jimmy takes about a half-dozen "trophy bucks" each season — and in a normal year two or three will measure above the B&C minimum. Odds like that simply don't occur with any of our other deer. Although there are very few outfitters who specialize in blacktails, Schaafsma isn't the only one who offers this kind of success on big blacktails — he's just the one I know best. Mind you, an outfitter like Schaafsma is not inexpensive on hunts for deer of this caliber. His leases cost a fortune, and of course those costs are passed along to his clients. There are high-dollar hunts for the other varieties of North American deer as well, and while the potential for a record-class specimen isn't quite so high, these special places do yield special deer. A significant difference is that blacktails are also democratic.

There are a fair number of wilderness areas and limited entry units that offer the same kind of odds for a really big blacktail... provided you're in good shape and willing to work hard to get him. So there's a choice. You can pay for your blacktail with a lot of research and plenty of sweat, or you can hire a good outfitter and pay in the coin of the realm, but either way, your chances of coming home with a really big buck are actually quite good. There are several reasons for this. One is that, in comparison with the other deer, the record-book minimum for blacktail is still relatively low. This is undoubtedly an offshoot of the general lack of interest in this deer; there are few serious trophy hunters who pursue blacktails, and over the decades very few big blacktailed deer have been measured.

Perhaps a more valid reason is that blacktails tend to have a much smaller home range than mule deer, so they can be managed well even on relatively small ranches. This does not happen, of course, on public lands that are accessible. However, limited entry units (Oregon has several good ones) and wilderness areas such as California's Trinity Alps and Yolla Bolly don't receive heavy hunting pressure, so the blacktailed bucks can mature and grow large.

A good example of the homebody nature of the blacktail is a buck they called "Rattler." He is not my best-scoring blacktail, but he's certainly my best buck. I can't tell you that it was a fabulous hunt; it was too short and too simple for that adjective. This was some years ago when Schaafsma was hunting a different ranch. Rattler hung out in the canyons and hills close by camp. He'd been big for several years, and so they'd tried to get him for several seasons. He had been fairly visible as well as recognizable, and was apparently a lot more lucky than smart. Over the seasons he had been missed several times, and even more frequently had somehow just slipped away.

I did not come to hunt Rattler. I hadn't even heard about Rattler, and Jimmy had never mentioned him because, for the first time in years, Rattler had not been seen. The assumption was that he had finally died of old age. But he hadn't. He was sleeping peacefully on a little oak-covered knoll not much more than 100 yards above the track to camp. It was the first or second day of my hunt, and we'd seen little that morning. We headed back out in the heat of the afternoon, and I doubt we were five minutes out of camp when Schaafsma glanced up the hill to his left and spotted him.

Schaafsma knew immediately that the bedded buck was Rattler. I didn't; I only knew that I was being told this was my buck by somebody who knows more about blacktails than anyone else I know. So I took a careful rest and shot Rattler, and he died peacefully in his bed. At that time he was at least 9-years old, possibly 10. Although he'd been a "book buck" in his prime, he was seriously downhill in the antlers now, with mismatched points but wonderful mass. He was not downhill in the body. We got him to a scale whole, and he weighed a whopping 180 pounds, a monster for a blacktailed deer.

In many ways it's unfortunate that I shot Rattler, for I surely didn't earn him, nor had I hunted him through the years. He does have a place of honor on my wall, and I hope I appreciate him properly. To this day some stranger will walk up to me at a sportsmen's convention and say, "You shot Rattler." And then I'll hear yet another story about how Rattler evaded an earlier bullet.

The Sitka blacktail deer is altogether different. In fact, so different that one of the few things it has in common with the Columbia blacktail is the black upper surface of the tail. This came as somewhat of a revelation to me. I'm not much of a "splitter" in the taxonomic scheme of things. I think we have too many caribou categories, and (as much as I love to hunt them) I've never fully understood why the Coues' whitetail, out of some 38 subspecies, is the only one singled out for a separate place in hunters' hearts and records books. So as soon as the Sitka blacktail was separated out as a record-book category I was not one of the guys who dashed up to Alaska to get one. It seemed to me a long way to go to hunt deer, especially with all of the other unique species that Alaska offers.

The only thing I was right about is that Alaska is a long distance to go for deer hunting. The Sitka blacktail is entirely different in both appearance and habit from the Columbia blacktail. He deserves his own place in the records book, for there is absolutely no correlation in antler size between the two mule deer subspecies. Moreover, the Sitka blacktail — at

The King David made an ideal camp; we anchored in a different cove every night and hunted different country every day.

the right place at the right time — offers the finest deer hunting in North America. And moreover still, the Sitka blacktail hunt is one of very few Alaskan hunts that can be taken on an unguided basis with every opportunity for an enjoyable and successful hunt.

As with Columbia blacktail, there are two good options for hunting Sitka blacktail: guided or unguided. Also as is the case with Columbia blacktail, prospective clients aren't exactly beating down the outfitters' doors. (The old "long way to go to hunt deer" syndrome.) However, virtually all the Kodiak bear outfitters do offer Sitka blacktail hunts. Prices are reasonable, especially as Alaskan hunting goes, and this is a very good option — perhaps better than you might think. Unguided is another sound option, but it is not quite as inexpensive as do-it-yourself hunting in the Lower 48.

You can hunt Sitka blacktails from the very limited Kodiak road system, which is by far the cheapest option. Some very fine bucks are taken this way, but understand that the concentrations of deer are generally found on the southern tip of the island, and no roads will take you there. So you need transportation and logistical support. No problem. There are plenty of air charter float planes in Kodiak that will drop you at a lake and pick you up a week later. Or, many of the commercial fishing boats take deer hunters in the fall. Charter planes are expensive and boats more so. However, to my mind the latter option is far the best. This is because you can use the boat as a camp, not only offering warm, dry quarters; but also providing a place you can bring your deer to where bears can't go.

To some extent it depends on the time of year. The season is very long, generally from August to the end of the year. In August and September most of the deer are usually high, well away from the beaches. At this time of year you are probably best-served by a float plane that will drop you off well inland. In October and early November the deer have usually moved down, so the boat option becomes much more viable. Beware of hunting later than mid-November. Sitka blacktails drop their antlers very early, and after mid-November you run the risk of a lot of antlerless bucks!

TOP: This Sitka blacktail deer is a big three-by-three with eye guards, with antlers very similar to a northeastern whitetail. This is arguably the best deer — of any variety — I have ever taken.
BOTTOM: In November, when the cover is down, you find Sitka blacktail deer out on the open slopes. It's ideal glassing country, and the numbers of deer are staggering.

This was the story on the first Sitka blacktail hunt I planned, which never actually happened. I was going up to hunt with Leon Francisco, a great brown bear outfitter, and the hunt was planned for around Thanksgiving. A few days before departure Leon called and canceled the hunt, telling me that it was an early winter and the bucks were shedding antlers like mad. I was disappointed, and to this day I've never met Leon Francisco (let alone hunted with him) — but I will never forget the professionalism required by that phone call.

A couple years later Jake Jacobsen called. Jake is an Alaskan Master Guide, but he's an Arizona native and we'd hunted Coues' deer together several times. Jake asked if I'd like to go Sitka blacktail hunting with him, not as a guide, but just to hunt together so he could collect some winter meat. It sounded good, and indeed it was.

We hunted with some friends of Jake's on the King David, a well-appointed salmon boat. From Kodiak we cruised to the southern tip of the island, catching some halibut and ling cod on the way. Thanks to the boat, we could anchor in a different inlet every night and hunt different country every day. It was a short hunt, just a week, and to date is my only experience with Sitka blacktail deer. However, I know I saw more than 500 bucks in that week!

Given that this was my only experience with this deer, this is what I think I learned. First, they're really different. At that time of year, early November, they were extremely visible on the open slopes — not at all cover-loving like the Columbian variety. Their body build is also altogether different. Well-adapted to their harsh climate, they are big-bodied deer that put on a lot of body fat. In profile they look like barrels with legs, much larger (at least on Kodiak) than any Columbian deer that walks. Live weights of 250 pounds are not unusual for mature bucks.

They have long hair, as you'd expect, and the capes are luxurious and colorful with the double white throat patch very common. Perhaps, unfortunately, their antlers are not so spectacular. The trick is to hunt them for what they are, not what you're used to or what you wish they could be (Coues' whitetails are much the same). I think I saw 500 bucks, certainly 100 bucks per day on the five days we could hunt. I know that I never saw a clean four-by-four. They exist, but are very rare. I saw two or three four-by-threes. One was a very nice buck and I shot him; the other two had the points, but nothing else. I doubt that I saw more than ten three-by-threes. I shot two of these. One was my first buck, a very nice typical "eight point-er" — three-by-three plus eyeguards. The other was my last buck, a real monster that easily exceeded the B&C minimum of 108 points. All the other 480-odd bucks were lesser animals; a few three-by-twos, a very few spikes, and hundreds of forkies of various persuasion.

The lesson here is that, at maturity, forked-horn antlers with eyeguards are probably normal for most Sitka blacktail bucks. It takes a lot of looking to find better, and it takes a lot of luck to find the clean four-by-four with eyeguards that we seek in other mule deer subspecies.

But what a hunt! I have never seen so many deer, nor so many bucks, nor had so much fun stalking them and sorting them out. Early on, in August and September, the brush is high and visibility is more limited. By November, when I hunt-ed, the cover was down and the deer were extremely visible. It was a glassing hunter's delight, with deer somewhere on virtu-ally every slope we glassed. The hunting was not easy, and it was cold, but it was a truly fabulous experience.

Although it's possible, and you hear a lot about it, we had no trouble with bears. The secret is to hunt in pairs and agree upon who has the shot. When a deer is taken, bone it on the spot, make up your packs, and walk away. The real danger comes from returning to a carcass the next morning. You real-ly don't want to do that, especially if the kill site is obscured by brush and you can't glass it from a safe distance!

The last deer I shot, the big one, came out of a little draw about 200 yards below us, and I just flat missed him. We relocated him, with some difficulty, far up on a bare slope. He was standing with a doe, and as we watched he bedded in the tall grass, now completely invisible. I traded my now-outdistanced .35 Whelen for Jake's .300 Winchester Magnum, and we waited. Finally he stood, facing us, and I held a few inches into the wind and shot for his white throat patch. That's where the bullet took him. To date he is my finest North American deer, and one of my most memorable shots. The aftermath was most memorable as well.

We had no sooner walked up to the deer than a big brown bear, hearing the shots like a dinner bell, appeared on the ridge above us. Fortunately this bear was a gentleman. He sat on his haunches, the wind rippling his long fur, and waited for us to finish our chores and make up our packs. Then we headed for the beach and he sauntered down the ridge to claim his share.

CHAPTER SIXTEEN ▪ BISON
An Echo From The Past

HUNTING THE BISON TODAY IS BUT A SHADOW OF WHAT ONCE WAS — BUT IN HIS PRESENCE YOU STILL HEAR THE THUNDERING HOOVES!

The American bison is an awesome animal. A big bull stands nearly as tall as a horse and weighs well over a ton. Heavy through the shoulders and distinctively hump-backed, he is one of the world's largest wild bovines, fully a quarter larger than Africa's famed Cape buffalo, larger than the Asian water buffalo. Only the legendary gaur, the Asian bison, is distinctly larger. With his woolly coat he is able to withstand the most brutal Great Plains winters. A herd animal, he uses his numbers to paw through the deepest snows to find grazing. Wolves will follow the herds and pick off the young, but the mature bison has no natural enemies, and he remains unchanged since long before man the hunter came onto the world's stage.

This, perhaps, is the bison's undoing. He is a creature of the wide open plains, and he never learned fear. His enemies were drought and desert, and his friends were grass and water over the horizon. He has close relatives, too; the European bison or wisent is virtually indistinguishable from the American breed. By the early years of this century the last major population of European bison had retreated into Poland's forests, and was nearly destroyed during World War II. Today the European bison exists in small private herds and preserves scattered across western Russia and eastern Europe — not unlike his American cousin. It is not known whether the European bison ever approached the numbers of his New World cousin. Perhaps, but not within the time of mankind. Throughout known history his numbers have been small. As we know, this was not the case with the American bison.

Just 140 years ago as many as 60 million bison roamed the Great Plains. He was the most numerous large mammal the world has ever seen, second in numbers only to man himself. Although our ***Records of North American Big Game*** now has its own history of some three-quarters of a century, and listed therein are many spectacular bison, we simply do not know how big the horns of this animal might potentially grow. Our records list only a smattering of heads that have survived from the 19th Century, and these few are from that century's last decade, long after the time of the bison was past. This does not denigrate the great bison listed in our book, but think of it like this: The few bison records that exist from the 1890s were taken from a remnant population of a few hundred animals. Those that are hunted today are taken from a still-remnant population of a few tens of thousands. What might the best bison horns have looked like when there were 60 million to choose among?

I suppose it doesn't matter, since we cannot turn back the clock, but wouldn't you like to see those mighty herds of bison stretching to the horizon? I'm a native Kansan, and I've never driven or bird-hunted through the Flint Hills or the endless plains to the west without imagining the time of the buffalo.

In paleologic time they were there for a very long time, and even in time as measured by man it seemed they would be there forever. But by both measurements they were gone in the wink of an eye. Lewis and Clark first made the East aware of the great herds of bison, although their extent remained long unknown and little believed. By the 1850s the existence of vast numbers of bison was both known and believed, but man's impact on the great herds was still small.

With the end of the Civil War and the coming of the railroad, the buffalo was doomed. Now there was unprecedented west-ward expansion, accelerated by rail access. Those same rails could transport hides and meat and buffalo tongues back to a hungry East. There were fortunes to be made in buffalo, and all too many headed West to cash in. An incredibly short 20 years after the Civil War, and the buffalo were finished.

The great Kansas herds, the most accessible due to the rail-road, went first. By the early 1870s they were gone. Then the "buffalo hunters" — quotes around both words, because bison are not buffalo and those who slaughtered them were not hunters as we know the term — turned south, eradicating the southern herds in Oklahoma and northern Texas in a few sea-sons. Then they turned to the northern bison, the last great herds. By the winter of 1884 it was over. A few survivors hung on here and there — along the Canadian border, in what became Yellowstone, and in the depths of the Black Hills. Theodore Roosevelt himself took one of the last South Dakota bison; you can read about it in his **Hunting Tales of a Ranchman** (1885).

By then the Great Plains were "pacified." Even if there were buffalo to return, there was no longer room for them. The last survivors in the breaks and badlands continued to be hunted for food, until finally protection came and our bison could begin the long road back from the brink of oblivion. The problem is that, unlike our whitetail, elk, wild turkeys, prong-horn, and so many other species that — with our help — have made a dramatic comeback, there is little room for the bison. He needs a lot of grass and space, and he's hard to fence in. Although there are many bison today, they are scattered in small private and public herds throughout their former range. And elsewhere.

There are bison farther east, west, north, and south than they ever occurred naturally — as far north as Alaska, as far south as central Mexico, and in the East as well. This is good, for it means there are bison somewhere close enough for most Americans to see, and we should all see this relic from a bygone era and remember how we destroyed him. It also means that there is more than adequate hunting opportunity, for virtually all of these small herds produce a surplus that must be har-vested — and most hunters, just like me, have a desire to relive the days of the buffalo, if only for a few moments.

The problem is that, again, the clock cannot be turned back. There is no bison hunting like what was seen in 1870, and there never will be again. Starting in 1977, the Boone and Crockett Records Committee accepts bison from the lower 48 states only for records, not for awards, and only from states that recognize the bison as wild and free-ranging, and for which a hunting license or big-game tag is required. This eliminates from the records a tremendous amount of bison hunting on pri-vate lands and Indian Reservations. In many cases this is good; some of the private-land "hunts" are little more than an execution. In fact, in all cases this is a good rule, for the B&C records book is based on generations of high standards, and they must not be relaxed for just one species. But sometimes this is unfortunate, for there are some very large private herds that, perhaps, offer some of the closest approximation to what might have been.

Regrettably, there are public hunts, too, that are little more than executions, with wardens or rangers pointing out the chosen animal. However, there are very good public hunts, too. Although not native, the Alaskan bison can offer a real hunt — and of course the hides are second to none. One of very best bison hunts is the free-ranging herd in Utah's Henry Mountains. As is the case in Alaska, it can take days to find the great beasts... and the shot must be taken in a spot where the butchering and recovery is possible. These, and others, are good hunts, not unlike the hunt Theodore Roosevelt enjoyed when he tracked a grand old bull in the Black Hills. But that's not what bison hunting was really like.

In fact, in those very few post-Civil War years, bison hunting wasn't hunting at all. The buffalo of Alaska's Farewell and Delta Junction herds, of Utah's Henry Mountains, and even the Black Hills survivors that Roosevelt hunted are anomalies, creatures that by luck or circumstances or sheer will learned to live in wooded, broken ground. The bison is a plains animal, and the plains wrote his glory and his doom. Except for a very few, the bison never learned to retreat into the mountains or trees. Except for a few, they never even learned to fight.

The bison is not a docile beast. Buffalo ranchers today have a terrible time keeping them within fences, and it isn't particularly uncommon for ranchers to get seriously hurt — occasionally killed — while working with the great, shaggy beasts. And yet there are very few accounts of bison charges from the old days, despite the fact that much of the shooting was done with inadequate blackpowder arms. This is in stark contrast to the vintage writing about hunting African buffalo, which was spiced with hair-raising escapades from the very beginning. Part of this, I think, stems from the fact that most bison hunting was done in very open country, where the game was always clearly visible and there were no surprises.

There is actually a scarcity of written records of the bison hunting. The African explorers were mostly educated men who began a long tradition of the great African hunting literature. This is largely lacking from our era of exploration. A few, like Alfred Mayer and Colonel Richard Dodge left accounts. Some, like Wild Bill Hickok and Buffalo Bill Cody, were popularized by the dime novels of the day, but you need more than a few grains of salt to swallow that genre! Mostly, I fear, our buffalo hunters

Colorado outfitter John Ray and I approach an exceptional plains bison, taken on a horseback hunt in southern Colorado.

were uneducated and often unsavory characters who made a living in a hard, dirty, bloody, and unsavory business. Chances are that many who could write saw nothing romantic enough to record in what they were doing... and their time passed so quickly that little remains but the legend.

That legend is of cool marksmen standing off from the herd with big Sharps rifles and dropping beast after beast with well-placed shots. Indeed that took place, but this was in the latter years of the buffalo hunting. In fact, the great Kansas herds were nearly eradicated before self-contained cartridges came into common use. Much of the buffalo hunting was done by a far different technique.

You will note that much of what vintage literature there is refers to the buffalo men not as "hunters" but as "runners." Until the availability of powerful rifles firing self-contained cartridges — in the early 1870s — the standard technique for buffalo hunting was to gallop a horse alongside and shoot at very close range. The Plains Indians were masters at this, and did it with both bow and, primarily, the buffalo lance. The buffalo "runners" did it with muzzleloaders, early low-powered repeaters like the Spencer, Henry, and "Yellowboy" 1866 Winchester, and with revolvers. The early African hunters, by the way, hunted elephant and rhino and Cape buffalo in exactly the same fashion.

There may be few accounts of bison charges, but this was seriously dangerous work. Needless to say, the horses would stampede the bison, and amid the swirling dust and shifting bodies the buffalo runners would draw alongside to take their shots. There was danger from the chosen bison, for one-shot kills were rare. There was danger from the other bison. And perhaps the greatest danger was from the horse stumbling in a prairie dog hole. George Custer himself accidentally shot and killed his wife's favorite horse when the steed stumbled and shifted his aim, and of course he was nearly killed by the fall.

Buffalo running was the favored technique until about 1875, when powerful breechloaders began making their way onto the plains. By now buffalo hunting was a narrow profit-and-loss venture, with cartridges counted carefully. Buffalo running was not only dangerous, but it spread the carcasses for miles and made the skinning time-consuming. With better rifles, the hunters found they could stand off from the herd — not 500 or 600 yards, but a couple hundred — and take several animals from a "stand" before the herd finally stampeded.

Without question these men were great marksmen. At the Battle of Adobe Walls, Billy Dixon is credited with knocking a Cheyenne off his horse at a half-mile. Their technique, however, was not exactly what you might think. We have a mental picture of the buffalo hunter — probably looking much like Tom Selleck in his "Quigley" attire — resting over his crossed sticks and making brain shot after brain shot. They probably didn't look — and certainly didn't smell — much like Tom Selleck. And the smart ones didn't even try brain shots.

The bison is a fairly placid, phlegmatic beast. He stampedes, and he charges, but he prefers to graze along at a leisurely pace. The buffalo hunters learned that they could place one of those big lead conical bullets through the lungs from a safe and comfortable distance, and the bison would continue to graze along until it fell over or lay down peacefully. They would often shoot several before the first one went down, and if the stand worked well the skinners could bring up the wagon and stay busy for hours in one place. It was not a pretty business, and it had no relationship to our modern sport hunting. It was borne out of a different era, a time of Manifest Destiny, shortsightedness, and political expediency. It is not a liberal myth that the demise of the bison was thought essential to conquer the Plains tribes; the Army, the railroad, the politicians, and the settlers were united in wishing to rid the plains of the bison and the Indians who lived on the plains. It's a wonder we didn't lose the bison altogether.

But we didn't. There will never again be 60 million bison, nor even one million, but there are many today. Enough that a bison hunt is easily arranged. Unless you are fortunate to draw a state tag, it is rarely inexpensive, but the cost is mitigated nicely by several hundred pounds of very fine meat! Even under the best circumstances a bison hunt is not a great hunt like most other North American hunts. Even where you must search for them bison aren't particularly hard to spot. Once spotted, they also aren't particularly hard to stalk. No, you can't walk up to a hunted bison herd, but you can usually get within rifle range without great difficulty. It is not like a stalk on a great ram or a fine buck or bull elk.

When you close on the herd, however, you can't help but feel transported to a long-gone time, and this feeling itself is worth experiencing. A mature bison bull, too, is a most awesome and impressive animal. You want to hunt him in winter, when his coat is at its fullest. Up close you'll be amazed at how thick and luxurious it is, and you'll understand why Americans of the horse-and-buggy era craved buffalo robes. The horns are not particularly large for so huge a beast... and you'll find that they are very difficult to judge.

A very big bison bull will have horns from about 16 to 18 inches in length, around the curve. Unlike most North American big-game animals, the final score doesn't reside so much in the length, but in the mass and how well it is carried through the horns. A really big bison may or may not have longer horns, but the basal circumference will be about the same as the length, and of course the thickness will hold up well through the length of the horn. That's all very well and good, except that this is the very devil to see on a bison. In this regard it's a lot like judging a muskox, an animal that I have more experience with than bison. On a muskox, the hair will almost always cover up the edges of the boss, so you have to take that on faith... and luck. On bison, even if you're unusually adept at judging circumference, you probably can't see the base of the horns in the thick hair.

In fact, with the prime winter coat that you really want to take a bison in, you often can't see much of the horns at all! What you can see is the general shape. You want horns that curve; straight horns may appear long, but you gain quite a bit of length along the curve. Most bison have a thick topknot of woolly hair on top of the skull, between the horns. If the horns have a nice curve and extend above that topknot, you're look-ing at good length. Then you have to see if the all-important circumference carries well through the horn.

The best thing is to try to look at a number of bison before you make a decision — preferably within a herd. This is not always possible with small, scattered herds. Sometimes the only option is to go on first impression, but with bison it's wise to compare as many animals as possible. With all animals there is a visual relationship between body size and horn size. For instance, the antlers of a 160-point whitetail look a lot different on a 140-pound Texas whitetail than they do on a 350-pound Canadian whitetail. You need to have some idea of the deer's body size in order to properly judge antlers. Bison are much the same, except it's even more difficult. The horns of a young, small-bodied bull will have about the same relationship to the head as the horns of a big, old bull... so look for body size first, and then start looking at horns. Bison with horns that come out from the skull and seem to turn upward with long, sharp tips are usually younger animals, while the older and bigger bulls seem to have more mass and curve than length. Like mountain goats, they are among our more difficult animals to judge — and very few of us will ever measure enough of them to become adept at it.

Shooting a bison is also not as simple as it sounds. They are huge and powerful animals; a body shot requires a big rifle and good bullet, but has the advantage of offering a huge vital zone. Because of the value of the meat, most guides will urge their hunters to take brain or neck shots. This is for two reasons. The obvious is that a head or neck shot ruins little meat, but equally important is that bison recovery is a big job, and it isn't simplified if the animal expires in the bottom of a gully or in thick timber! It sounds easy, but is actually extremely difficult... especially since, again, this isn't 1870 and few of us will ever shoot enough bison to get it right.

The neck shot is difficult because of the wild hair, and also because the spine drops low through the neck and then curves back up to join at the shoulders. It's easy to miss. The brain shot is tricky because all that thick hair obscures aiming points. Sometimes you can't even see the ears! The brain actually rests very high in the skull, and it's easy to miss, too. Which is exactly what I did when I shot my first bison.

I was on the Pine Ridge Sioux Reservation in South Dakota, and game manager Richard Sherman talked me through it. It was really a very nice hunt; we looked at quite a few bison from a distance, and when we made our choice we crawled in fairly close. I was very steady, the presentation was good, and I had time to think the shot through and make sure I was holding on the right spot. None of this mattered; I still shot too low, and the bull gave little notice whatsoever. Well, that's not true. He merely shook his head, then launched into high gear. I was shooting a Winchester Model '71 in .348 Winchester, and I had expected it to be plenty of gun. Had I shot where I was supposed to it probably would have been. As it was, I put three more 250-grain Barnes bullets into the lungs as the bull ran... all with no apparent effect. He was with a little herd, and they ran up over a low hill and vanished. The rest kept going; my bull was in a grassy bowl on the far side, already going down when I got to the top.

When I walked up to him I was astounded at his size, and I recognized that I'd underestimated not only the size, but also the strength of this great animal. It was altogether my fault that I missed the brain shot, but, having done so, I didn't have nearly enough gun to properly finish the job! There are two approaches, and either is perfectly appropriate. You could use a scope-sighted "conventional" hunting rifle, relying on the scope to make absolutely certain of a first-round brain shot. Or you could use a large rifle with a big, heavy bullet.

The second time I hunted bison I used a more traditional setup, a single-shot .45-70, using blackpowder loads with hard-cast lead bullets. This was in southern Colorado with John Ray of Thousand Hills Bison Ranch. I didn't get fancy; I tried for the traditional lung shot, and although that first big bullet didn't put him down, it absolutely anchored him. I think I could have left him, and in a short time he would have laid down and expired. But we modern hunters aren't built that way any more, so I kept shooting until he went down! He was a magnificent bull with more than 20 inches of thick horn on each side, a relic from a bygone age. When I first saw him standing alone in a little sagebrush valley I could imagine what it must have been like when his kind blanketed the plains.

CHAPTER SEVENTEEN ▪ THINHORNS
The Thinhorn Sheep

NORTHWESTERN CANADA AND ALASKA HOLD THE WORLD'S
MOST AVAILABLE WILD SHEEP... AND THEY OCCUPY SOME
OF THE MOST MAGNIFICENT COUNTRY.

The thinhorn sheep of the far North have always been very
special to me, and for many reasons. Like all hunters of my gen-
eration, I grew up devouring the works of Jack O'Connor, so of
course I knew that sheep hunting was superior to all other
forms of the sport. It was the 1960s, and O'Connor was growing older. By then his days of hunting bighorns, both the desert
sheep of Sonora and the Rocky Mountain rams of Alberta, were
long since over. The sheep hunting he was writing about was
Dall's sheep in the Yukon and Stone's sheep in the Cassiars...
and he made those mountains come alive for me and millions of
young hunters just like me.

Unlike many, however, I was very fortunate; my dreams of
those northern mountains didn't have to percolate in my sub-
conscious for decades. In 1973, over 30 years ago now, my dad
and I went to the Cassiars. Although we had hunted deer and
pronghorns and elk and such, this was my first "big hunt," so of
course the memory remains special. We went into Frank Cooke's
Scoop Lake camp right on the heels of Jack and Eleanor
O'Connor, who had just completed one of their last sheep hunts.
This, too, made it special.

But what really made it special and keeps the memory bright
to this day, was the magnificence of northern British Columbia.
There had been good rains that summer, and the high basins
were emerald green. The leaves were just turning, and the
heather and alder bottoms striped the hills with swaths of yellow
and crimson. I have been many places since, but I have yet to
see country that matches the Cassiar Mountains in early fall.

Come to think of it, I have yet to see game that matches the
magnificence of the rams that live there. We all have our

favorites, of course. The snow-white sheep to the north are beautiful, and the bighorns to the south are awesome. Each variety of antlered game has its own special attraction, and the bears are dramatic creatures. Perhaps oddly, I do not consider myself a "sheep hunter," but I have long maintained that the dark pepper-and-salt sheep of northern British Columbia are the most gorgeous creatures in North America — and the most beautiful wild sheep in the world.

I suspect, like many of us, for most of my life I assumed that the dark sheep of northern British Columbia and adjacent southern Yukon were named after the gray and black rocks they live among. Actually, they're named after an early naturalist named Stone, so they are properly Stone's sheep, capitalized and possessive. Likewise, the pure white sheep to their north are named after a fellow named Dall, so they are properly Dall's sheep.

In the early days it was thought that these two wild sheep, so distinctly different in appearance, were altogether different species of sheep. In fact they are not; they are, respectively, *Ovis dalli dalli* and *Ovis dalli stonei,* the two primary subspecies of our thinhorned wild sheep. Although the Stone's sheep is slightly larger and has the potential to grow slightly larger horns, the primary difference is color — Stone's sheep in the heart of their range are very dark, and Dall's sheep are pure white. This, of course, is a problem for the animals; they only know that they are sheep, neglecting to indulge in the color distinctions we humans are prone to. There is, therefore, a fairly broad intergrade area in south-central Yukon, where sheep in a given band may range from more-or-less white to more-or-less gray. These are the so-called Fannin's sheep, which, at their most classic, are very light in color with a dark saddle patch, but they can actually be any shade or mixture of white with a sprinkling of dark hairs.

To keep things simple, most record-keeping systems decree that Dall's sheep are pure white, while thin-horned sheep with dark hairs mixed into the white are Stone's sheep. Historically this has never caused a problem; although a few dark hairs may occasionally be found, the sheep of Alaska are white, as are the sheep of the Mackenzies in Northwest Territories. The sheep of northern British Columbia are dark — except for a

The range of southern and central Alaska are often extremely rugged. This is Dall's sheep country in the Wrangell's; the ram I shot was spotted from here, but he was over on the next mountain. Getting to him and back again on foot was a really long day.

small band of Dall's sheep in that little northwestern corner around Atlin, north of Skagway, Alaska. The sheep of western, northern, and even far eastern Yukon are also white Dall's sheep, with the only area of contention being a relatively small region east of Whitehorse and north of the British Columbia line. This is the primary transition zone, split between just a small handful of outfitters.

It's an irony of history that these have become some of the most desirable hunting territories in North America. In the earlier years of serious sheep hunting these Yukon outfitters could hardly give their sheep away; they weren't pure white, only rarely were they the very classic dark Stone's, and few were the collectors who really wanted the unrecognized Fannin's sheep. Things changed. The white Dall's sheep occupy a huge range, from the Mackenzies clear across the Yukon and on to western Alaska, found in most mountain ranges throughout. They are quite possibly the most numerous wild sheep in the world, and to this day there is little human encroachment into their habitat.

The Stone's sheep occupies one of the more limited ranges of the world's wild sheep. They are found only in the northern third of British Columbia, straddling the Rocky Mountain Trench into the ranges on both sides; and a bit farther north into the Yukon. In the 1950s and into the 1960s this was not a problem; northern British Columbia was huge and remote, and there were lots of sheep for those adventurous enough to reach them. In that era the Stone's sheep was very likely to be the last leg of the journey to the Grand Slam.

Things changed rapidly. The cult of sheep hunting grew, egged on by the matchless writing of Jack O'Connor. The number of hunters in search of the Grand Slam grew as well. In his later years O'Connor regretted this tremendously, but (despite rumor and legend) it was not he who coined the phrase. That distinction goes to Grancel Fitz, who was among the first to accomplish the feat. In answer to the sheep fever, and helped by the proliferation of floatplanes, good outfitters fully penetrated B.C.'s limited Stone's sheep range. By the early 1970s the Stone's sheep was the most available of all the wild sheep. The Stone's sheep was my first ram on the journey to the Grand Slam. Given the current availability of desert bighorns, I am amazed that I was able to complete it 30 years later! But that 1973 Stone's sheep was a wonderful start.

There's a story there. In 1973 a mixed-bag hunt in B.C. was my graduation present from college. Dad must have had faith that I would graduate; the present was a year early, since I'd be going off to the Marines as soon as I got my diploma. Jack Atcheson set it up for us, a moose-caribou-goat hunt in the Cassiars. A sheep hunt would have been a bit more costly, but not much, so at some point I asked Jack — still my friend and mentor after all these years — if there was a possibility. He recommended that I show up in camp with a tag (the cost was $25 back then!) and talk to the outfitter. I was just a couple of weeks out of Officer Candidate School, and after a decade of long-haired American draft dodgers, old Frank Cooke liked me. Or at least he liked my haircut. Pop talked to him, and he allowed that I could have a Stone's sheep for $500 — provided I'd agree to take a nice ram, but not one of his big ones.

A few days later my Indian guide and I glassed two rams feeding a short distance from a long chute that ran from the basin we were in almost to the top of the mountain. We bailed off our mounts, and I'll never forget the lesson I learned when, leaving the horses and dashing the short distance to the cover of the chute, he said, "Sheep can't count."

We toiled up through the steep rocks, overshooting the rams by a significant margin. Even at that, the shot wasn't difficult. At least the first shot wasn't, but I missed him clean, and the second shot, as he ran through the heather ahead of the lesser ram, was one of my most memorable.

I regret very much not hunting that country and those rams more than I have, but things changed quickly. Too many nonresidents were taking too many sheep, and for the first time there was significant resident hunting pressure as well. By 1975, trophy quality was dropping dramatically. The British Columbia game department, in a move that was most unpopular, but absolutely necessary, instituted a quota system. For most outfitters this cut the number of rams they could take to a half or a third of what they had been taking — and prices skyrocketed.

It has taken many years, but today there are more big Stone's sheep seen — and taken — than since the late 1960s. Unfortunately the nonresident quotas remain very tight as resident hunting pressure has continued to escalate. Not only are B.C. Stone's sheep hunts very expensive, but it can be a matter of some years to get a booking in the better areas. This, obviously, has created wonderful opportunity for the few Yukon outfitters who could offer dark-haired sheep! Historically the Yukon rams run a bit smaller, but with much lighter pressure and the rams having a chance to live longer — not to mention more available and somewhat less expensive hunts — Yukon Stone's sheep outfitters have done very well the last couple of decades, and good for them!

I will not pretend to be an expert on hunting our thin-horned sheep. I have hunted them just six times, four times for Dall's and twice for Stone's. However, from this limited perspective I do have some opinions on the hunting of them. First off, hunting wild sheep differs very little the world over. The *Ovis* genus is not a creature of the high, slick rocks like the goat, genus *Capra*. He is a creature of grassy bowls and Alpine meadows. However, the hunting does differ because within that framework the altitudes and vegetation differ dramatically.

Having been fortunate enough to have drawn good bighorn tags, and also having broken my back and my heart in Montana's "unlimited permit" country, and having done some sheep hunting in Asia, it is my opinion that most sheep are not nearly so difficult to hunt as most deer. They see well, but in general are not nearly so wary as the deer of the world. The secret the world over is first finding them, and then getting close enough for a shot. The difficulty of doing either varies with the terrain, the relative density of the sheep, and probably the hunting pressure they have endured.

Bighorns, for instance, are legendary for their craftiness and their propensity to stay in timber. Given pressure and/or warm weather, this is true. But take a good limited-permit area and some cool weather, and bighorns are much easier to hunt than the thinhorned sheep. But add in some hunting pressure, warm weather, and a relative scarcity of sheep, and bighorns are exceedingly difficult.

Now, with most thinhorn sheep hunting you can take away the timber. When it gets warm the sheep — especially the Stone's sheep — will stay in the brush and be difficult to find, but not nearly so difficult as bighorns under similar circumstances. Of course it depends on the mountains. My second

TOP: A backpack sheep camp in the Yukon's Bonnet Plume Range, exceptionally steep and rugged country that holds good numbers of mature rams.
BOTTOM: My very best Dall's sheep was taken in the Yukon's Bonnet Plume Range in 1999. Just shy of 40 inches, this heavy-horned, perfectly shaped ram was 11-1/2 years old, a great trophy.

Stone's sheep hunt was a foot hunt in the Skeena Mountains of northwestern B.C., and in an area that had been developed very little. The lower slopes were a jungle of thick brush and devil's club, impassable to a horse and virtually so for a man. On the second day from last we finally found a band of rams far, far up a steep-sided valley. We might have reached them in two hard days, and we might not have, but we couldn't have gotten back. So I watched them through the spotting scope for several hours, just little wiggling worms across the great distance that I could not cross.

It is my opinion that, today, hunting Stone's sheep is more difficult than hunting Dall's sheep. Because they are farther south, there is more brush. Thirty years ago, given time and effort, success on a big ram was virtually assured. There are more big rams than there were 25 years ago, but today — and perhaps forever — big Stone's rams are scarce and take lots of looking. The looking is not difficult. Stone's sheep are indeed colored like the rocks, but they don't live in rocks. You'll find them in the high saddles and basins, and they're not so difficult to glass — not nearly so difficult as bighorns. Although heavy brush is a problem, most of the mountains they live in are neither especially high nor especially rugged; horseback hunts remain the most common, a big plus for covering ground and seeing country.

When you move north into white sheep country the timberline drops in elevation, and the tops become, if not necessarily higher, more barren. This is an important distinction because nothing, but nothing, is as easy to glass as Dall's sheep. Reaching them can be a different story, but even Stevie Wonder could glass Dall's sheep. Rocky Mountain goats, especially billies, tend to be off-white and can be confused with pale rocks. With Dall's sheep there is no question, ever. They show up like salt crystals mixed with pepper, and you can see them from distances much too great to ever get to, let alone judge horns.

This does not make them easy to hunt; it just makes them easier to see. With sheep, of course, that's half the battle. Having said that, it was only recently that I finally took a "big" Dall's sheep — and he remains the only ram I have ever seen that approaches the magical "40-inch" mark. He was a 12 1/2-year-old ram, with good bases and perfectly matched horns just under 40 — so I guess I've never actually seen a genuine 40-inch ram! They're there, but they aren't easy to find.

Horseback hunts are relatively common in the Yukon, but most of Alaska and the Mackenzies are too remote to bring in horses for the season — and the winters far too harsh to keep them there. Horseback hunting has a significant advantage in that you can cover much more ground, and the more country you can glass the better your chances of seeing a big ram. On the other hand, country that is accessible to horseback has often been hunted hard, and the older rams may be somewhere out of cayuse country.

This is not to say that backpacking is necessarily the best option. Dall's sheep show up well at great distances, but they live in huge country and aren't exactly on every hillside. I generally prefer backpack or foot hunting because with horses, no matter what happens you must sooner or later come back to them — and that may not be the direction you wish to go. However, hunting the northern mountains on foot is tough stuff. They may not be especially high, but they are often very rugged and they're certainly very big. It isn't for everybody, nor is it automatically the best course to a big ram. This depends on luck, as well as on effort and persistence.

There's also a psychological difficulty with foot hunting, even if you're in pretty good shape. Sooner or later, no matter how much discipline you want to have, you may reach a point where a ram is going to bite the dust. A number of years ago I hunted the Wrangells in eastern Alaska, a rugged and dramatically beautiful range. Early in the hunt we spotted three rams far across an impossible canyon. Two were beyond full curl, one tight and the other flared. That was about all we could tell; the distance was horrendous.

We moved on the rams before first light. In August in Alaska this was about 2 a.m. They were on a very steep sidehill, a series of rocky chutes. We got there by mid-morning, but of course the rams had moved. We sidehilled along, slipping in the steep shale — and then the wide-horned ram stepped out on a rocky point above us. By then the commitment was made; I took a snap shot and missed him.

Now the commitment was really made; I'm not sure we ever looked at the horns again! But we sure did keep hunting him! The three rams headed out, and between following tracks and getting the occasional glimpse we stayed with them. About four o'clock in the afternoon we finally caught them crossing a little shale slide. I shot the wide-horned ram that I was fixated on, and my partner shot the other ram, a full-curl with a deeper curl and heavier horn. Neither was a monster, but his ram — the one I never gave a second glance — was actually better than mine.

This didn't matter. Both were lovely rams, but neither was as big as I had hoped for — and I had more than a week left to hunt. I should have looked more closely before we passed the "point of no return." By the way, the other part of the equation is that it was now five o'clock in the evening and we had two sheep to pack out. Dark caught us about midnight, and we huddled by a pale willow fire for two hours before trudging on in twilight. We stumbled back to camp sometime in the late morning, at the end of the longest hunting day I've ever spent.

Nearly a decade later I went on another backpack hunt with Arctic Red River in the Mackenzies of Northwest Territories. That season opens in July, when the sheep are slick and sleek in their summer coats. The grassy slopes are emerald green, and the weather is mild. If you're man enough you can hunt from about two in the morning until past midnight, just taking a little break when the light becomes too dim for glassing. On a backpack hunt, chances are good you won't hold that schedule for more than a day or so!

Thinhorn sheep seem to follow the pattern of most wild sheep, being much more active in the evening than during the early morning hours. So my guide, Stu Langlands, and I would normally sleep as long as we could in the mornings, often not leaving our spike camp until well after noon. Once out, though, we'd hunt through the afternoon and evening, generally stumbling back into camp during that brief period of semi-darkness.

We saw sheep and legal rams every day. But the days passed and we never, ever saw the kind of ram I was looking for — and that the area normally produces. I was warned about this; outfitter Kelly Haugen told me that the bigger rams usually don't appear until mid to late August. It wasn't that I disbelieved him, but where would they appear from? The mountains are there,

TOP: Provided the weather cooperates just a bit, most hunts for both Dall's and Stone's sheep are successful. This was the result of a Mackenzie Mountain hunt with Arctic Red River: three hunters, three rams.
BOTTOM: In the northern mountains fog banks are often a real problem for sheep hunters. When the fog sets in, visibility goes away and there's usually little choice but to wait it out.

and the sheep are in the mountains, so surely we would see the sheep that were there.

When a good outfitter gives you his best suggestion, take it! Within two weeks of the completion of my hunt — in mid-August —three rams over 40 inches were taken from that area. I never saw one close to that, although as the hunt drew to a close I had looked at an awful lot of rams. We were down to about a day and a half left, and Stu wanted to keep looking. A better man — or better hunter — than I probably would have kept looking, but I let the pressure of stories to write and time slipping away get to me. We spotted a very pretty heavy-horned ram far across a deep valley, and I shot him after a lovely stalk brought us within 60 yards. I don't regret it; I'd long wanted a Dall's sheep in that shiny summer coat, but next time I'll go when the outfitter tells me to go!

It was September of '99 when I took my big Dall's sheep. This was in Richard Rodgers' Bonnet Plume country in the Yukon. I had envisioned the same kind of gentle green mountains I'd hunted in Northwest Territories, but the Bonnet Plume range in east-central Yukon is abrupt and jagged, as rugged as any sheep country I've ever seen. It was a tough hunt, but not a long one; we hiked up from a base camp and, just before dark, glassed several rams at long range. We moved on them in the morning, and late that afternoon I shot the kind of Dall's ram I'd always wanted.

Dall's sheep remain our most available wild sheep — perhaps in the world, as well as North America. More and more Alaskan areas are going to permit draws, and there is more and more resident pressure as Alaska's population increases. But there remains a great deal of fine sheep hunting in Alaska, enough that costs for guided sheep hunts haven't escalated nearly as much as they have for, say, moose and the big bears. Most of Alaska's mountains, from the Chugach in the south to the Brooks in the north, hold good sheep, but Alaska is not the only place to hunt Dall's sheep. The Yukon remains very good, and the Mackenzies are very good. All things considered, I don't think one area is better than another, but the circumstances are different.

Many outfitters in the Yukon use horses, a few do in the Mackenzies, and still fewer are able to use them in Alaska. An Alaskan hunt is likely to be a single-species, sheep-only hunt, while a Yukon hunt (with horses) is more likely to be a mixed bag affair. Later on in my Yukon hunt I took a nice caribou, and I saw a couple of decent moose as well. In the Mackenzies it depends on the circumstances. I could have taken a mountain caribou, for instance... but if you take other game on a backpack sheep hunt the hunt is over for several days! In any case, if you want a good ram the best option is to just hunt sheep. Check references carefully and find both an outfitter and a guide who are sheep hunters. Dall's sheep are plentiful enough across most of their range that this is far more important than where you choose to hunt.

The options for hunting Stone's sheep remain few: Classic areas in British Columbia or those few territories in adjacent Yukon. If a Stone's sheep is on your dream list, save your pennies and do it as soon as you can. Costs continue to escalate and quotas continue to tighten, and I don't see it getting better. I still rate a dark pepper-and-salt Stone's sheep as the most attractive of the world's wild sheep, and his mountains as some of the prettiest country on Earth. I'd love to hunt him again—but the reality is that I may have to stand on that one ram. I'm satisfied to do that if I must. I remember that day and those mountains like it was yesterday, and that first ram remains one of my most prized trophies.

*Following is a bonus chapter written by
Craig Boddington's uncle, Arthur
Popham, who is mentioned throughout
this book. This chapter originally
appeared in* Outdoor Life, *and is part of
Popham's,* **Stalking Game from Desert
to Tundra**, *published by Amwell Press
in 1985.*

---

*Arthur C. Popham grew up in Kansas City,
Missouri. All through high school there he did
much target and small game shooting with high
power rifles and pistols, and got his first taste of
deserts and mountains in his freshman college
year at New Mexico Military Institute in Roswell.
At 17, he bagged his first deer on a
Thanksgiving holiday hunt out of Alamogordo.*

*In his junior college year, Art went to the
University of Arizona at Tucson, and nearly
every weekend was spent in the deserts and
mountains with such game-and-gunwise men-
tors as Jack O'Connor and George Parker, Jr.,
whom he idolized.*

*Art became a member of the Boone and Crockett
Club in 1960.*

CHAPTER EIGHTEEN
Ram from Inferno by Arthur C. Popham

HIGH-FLYING FISH IN THE DESERT WAS ONLY ONE OF THE MANY INCIDENTS OF THIS WEIRD TRIP INTO A FIERY FURNACE...

I was enjoying a cool vacation from college, surrounded by Minnesota's 10,000 limpid lakes, when Jack O'Connor's telegram came from Tucson, Arizona. He was inviting me to join him on a desert sheep hunt arranged with Charlie Ren, then the aging dean of the desert hunters. Before September classes started at the University of Arizona was our only chance for a crack at those rare trophies; then Jack's duties in teaching journalism and mine in learning law resumed. So I headed eagerly for Tucson to meet him, little realizing how I'd soon be gasping for just one cupful of all that clear, cool water I left behind.

This was too many years ago, before the desert bighorns in Mexico's arid mountains were so nearly wiped out by waterhole slaughters, and before their hunting was totally prohibited there.

The renaissance, meanwhile, of the Rocky Mountain and desert bighorn sheep is another fine chapter in the saving of our North American game animals. Good management of the wild herds in the Western states has made possible again their limited open seasons, and Mexico has recently permitted the taking of some desert sheep in the Baja California area after long protection.

Harvesting the older animals under these allotted permits has now become a well-organized operation in some areas for private outfitters and guides, pitting aerial spotting, four-wheel-drive vehicles and walkie-talkie communication between spotters

Art Popham photographed by his Kansas City, Missouri, boyhood friend, David Douglas Duncan, while they knocked around Arizona together as college students. This was one of Duncan's first prize-winning pictures — before he became world-famous as a photojournalist for Life *magazine and others.*

against the sheep's telescopic eyesight, protective coloring and fearless agility in its rough habitat.

This has all brought to mind the very different kind of hunt for desert bighorns that we made. It had actually been Jack's fascinating articles in the early 1930s on southwestern hunting that had drawn me to the University of Arizona as a student, where he was then a young faculty member. I'd lost little time after enrolling in getting acquainted with him; we hunted Kaibab Forest mule deer together on that Thanksgiving vacation, and shot together for desert game through the year. Jack has gone on, of course, to become one of the outstanding authorities on world big game hunting and guns, and I have long enjoyed the extracurricular education I received with him then.

So, in response to his telegram, I met Jack in Tucson that August, and we rolled through the shimmering mirages to Ajo, Arizona. There, Charlie Ren, a lean old desert hawk, met us and assembled our gear and party in a vintage Dodge pickup truck and Ford sedan. We cleared at the border, then headed south toward the ranges paralleling the Gulf of California.

Our group was filled out by Roy Graham, deputy sheriff at Ajo. Charlie's right-hand man was Jose del Rosario, a young redheaded Mexican, who was to be my guide. I don't know if Red's coloring reflected Mayan or Irish influence, but he knew the desert, had marvelous eyesight and was a keen hunter.

After a day's travel we ran out of ruts to follow and picked our way over the desert around the cactus. Cholla thorns, always lying in wait for tires, produce slow leaks that are aggravatingly persistent. The vehicles took a beating as we pushed our way in the scorching glare, scraping through the greasewood and spiny ocotillo, past stately saguaro and organ cactus, churning through dry washes. Sangre grado trees, with elephant-colored bark, looked heavy and strong, but were easily snapped. Filled with staining red juice, they went down before the bumper like neck-shot deer.

The boiling radiators took more and more of our precious water supply. Charlie planned to refill the five-gallon cans at a water seep he knew that lay near the surface. This was used by the Seri Indians occasionally, and Charlie found the spot all right. But there we received our first body-blow. The shallow wells were bone dry!

The situation was saved by a rip-snortin' thunderstorm that reached us after midnight. In the glare of the lightning we saw the desert hardpan quickly become a lake as the rain lashed down in the crashing thunder. We finished the night in the cars, sandwiched between the top and our hastily dumped-in gear.

Our course next morning lay across a big arroyo. Dusty the night before, it was now brimful with a roaring torrent from the flash flood. So we boiled a big pot of Mexican frijoles and waited for the river to subside. Seri Indians had camped there ahead of us, and the shells of many roasted tortoises lay about. The run-off from the hard ground was so rapid that by late afternoon it was down to a shallow flow, and we were able to get the vehicles across. Meanwhile we had gratefully filled the water cans with the precious muddy fluid that was both our salvation and delay.

Pushing on southward, we reached a broad basin where the rain had formed a shallow lake several hundred yards across. There was a range of mountains within reach to hunt, so we unloaded where we had water and set out to look for sheep sign.

Bouncing over the desert in the steaming, laden cars had been hot, but climbing all day on the barren, scorching rocks with no shade to be found even for a brief respite proved far more punishing. We found that our bodies' built-in, evaporative cooling systems worked amazingly well, as long as the water intake was ample. With the great exertion of climbing, a man had to consume at least a gallon a day to keep going. Even at that rate, and more, it was all lost by perspiration so that we needed no urinary systems.

And what were we pumping through our pores at such a rate? It was the fluid from our big mud puddle at camp, and was just the color of coffee with lots of cream. I would squeeze a little lime juice in a cupful, which seemed to help settle the mud into the lower half, and sip off the top part. We must have had beautiful insides, with all that mud pack treatment!

While we lay in the cooling nights, Charlie Ren told us much of his desert sheep hunting lore. He pointed out that sound and scent travel upward from the canyons as well as in the rising air along the heated mountainsides, and he emphasized the advantage of getting above the sheep to hunt them. But, tied to our water supply, we couldn't get our camp closer than about three miles from the base of the mountains. This meant six miles of worthless walking over the desert in the heat every day. With the scant cover, of course any sheep on our side of the mountain would see us coming from afar. They would be long gone over to the other side before we even started the climb of three or four-thousand feet. This meant that our only chance lay first in getting far up on our side of the mountain, higher than any sheep that might be on the other side. Then we could ease around the top and try to spot them from above.

With the warm nights, the simple strategy would have been to lie out overnight on the mountain, to be above any moving sheep at daylight. But we couldn't carry enough water to be away from the source that long and make it back to camp!

So for three days we camped by our dwindling rain pool, walked to the mountain, clambered over the hot rocks and found only some old sheep droppings. I did see one ewe, after I'd spent half a day working up from the valley floor. I lay panting in the sparse shade of a cactus, and watched her pick her way easily up the same mountainside, covering the distance in about ten minutes. That's when you wonder what the heck a mere human animal is doing out on a mountain trying to make like a wild sheep!

By then our big mud puddle had shrunk almost to a dried flat. As it receded, an object in the middle became identifiable as a long-dead horse. No doubt his essence had added considerable strength to that steaming, earthy broth, but we hastily decided to move!

We were less than a day's travel from the Gulf of California shore. With so little encouragement in these first mountains, our lust for rams had become a little desiccated, along with everything else. The idea of feeling a cooling breeze from the water was more than we could stand, so we headed for the coast. Finally coming over a ridge and rolling over the parched land toward a broad beach, nothing ever looked better than that blue water reaching to the horizon! Yes, it was salty; we couldn't drink it, but compared to the cracking mud flat we'd left, just the sight of the clear, translucent water lapping at our feet was enough to bring a tear to the eye.

We lost little time in plunging into the wet coolness to soak our dried-out hides. Small fish, flashing in the sun, darted about us. Then as I waded along, chasing them, something brushed between my legs. Glancing down, I was startled to see it was a stingray. Mindful of the reputed paralyzing pain of its tail stinger, I lost equally little time in seeking shallower water!

Lack of meat had become a serious problem to us. We could carry no fresh meat, of course, without refrigeration, and in our heavy exertion in climbing felt the need of it badly. Efforts to bag an incidental deer, as planned, had not worked out.

Now we watched big, plump-breasted curlews feed in shifting flocks along the beach. There was a dinner worth trying for! We roamed up and down the shore with the shotgun, but had no cover of any kind. The only stalking possible was a pretended indifference. The birds must have seen the hungry gleam in our eyes, for those tantalizing tidbits would never let us within range.

We saw fish of every kind rolling and jumping just off shore. Such tempting sea fare! Without boat or tackle, we could only watch them wistfully and drool.

In the midst of this frustration, I had noticed a great osprey with its nest in a tall saguaro cactus a quarter-mile inland. It had a regular route high over the blazing desert to the shore. There the powerful hawk would poise over the water, then plummet in out of sight, to rise with a shining fish in its talons. Carrying its prey headfirst, like a pontoon slung below it, the bird would take the meal to the nest, and soon return for another.

In desperation, I stationed myself below the osprey's flight path and waited. Sure enough, over it came with a gleaming fish. I peppered the high-flying bird with shot, and the osprey flared, dropping the shiny prey. Running to the spot, I exultantly scooped up a fresh, 15-inch mullet from the burning desert sand. Roasted brown, my finny shotgun trophy made a grand dinner I'll never forget. That must be a record of some sort for shooting down the highest-flying fish!

Our beach was opposite Tiburon Island, about three miles out in the Gulf of California. It was the stronghold of the Seri Indians. They are recognized as probably the most primitive people on our continent, living under great privation. I'd heard many stories of their indelicate tastes as they scavenged the beaches for food, as well as their feats of running down mule deer on the rocky desert island they called home. They had camped about our location, as evidenced by more of their roasted tortoise shells, but none appeared while we were there. Though we'd brought bright trade goods to establish friendly relations with any we met, we were as happy not to have any of their uninhibited members around!

We had looked forward to a cool, pleasant night on the shore after the sun's torch died, envisioning a sea-fresh breeze to lull us by the lapping waves. Our sweet dream turned into a nightmare that left us all stupefied by morning!

First, I was bitten by a blisterbug. A red-hot needle hit me in the chest, and the spot spread to a fiery splotch the size of a dinner plate, with an incandescent blister in the middle. Believe me, those insects are potent!

Then the breeze died completely. The moist sea air mingled with the desert's radiant heat, and a stifling blanket of humidity settled upon us. The discomfort was increased by our bodies' briny coating from the swimming, there being none of our precious "fresh" water for rinsing. And then the sand fleas took over. There was a night straight from purgatory!

By dawn we were all in such murderous humor that we almost feared speaking to each other. With common consent, we dully loaded up the cars and headed inland for a red mountain seen on the shoreward trek. Charlie had found sheep there before, and our spirits rose as we rode. After our experience on the shore, we could appreciate better the dryness of the desert air, and how its evaporative cooling made the heat bearable.

With camp set up at the base of the long, typical up-slope to the foot of the red mountains, we got down to business next morning. An early start was always a necessity. The dawn hours before the sun hit were precious for the long walk up the sloping foothills, or bajada, to the mountain's steep base.

Those were the memorably delightful times of the trip. The desert cools off rapidly at night; by dawn we were chilly in shirtsleeves before swinging along over the dewy sand. There was often the fresh track of a ghostly mule deer to follow hopefully toward the high ground, but in the washes and gullies running from the slopes not one ever offered a shot. Usually, after starting up the mountain, we could pick them up far below us with the glasses, standing silvery grey in the shade of a bent-armed saguaro.

The long, pleated arms of some of the pitaya cactus bore a coral colored, plum-sized fruit. These were scarce, and always grew on the west side of the trunks, so even after the sun was well up, the fruits would be shaded. It was sheer delight to find one fresh and cool in the growing heat, break open its waxy, watermelon-red interior flecked with tiny black seeds, and savor the lush ambrosia.

In proper season I love the desert dearly, with all its unsuspected life, activity and color. Many years after this trip of ours I had the privilege of working much with the late Grancel Fitz, dedicated North American big game hunter and co-author of the scoring system, judging for the Boone and Crockett Club Records Committee the continent's top trophies. I was most intrigued to learn that he, too, had made a desert sheep hunt with the outfitter Charlie Ren, but, more sensibly, in November of that same year. As Grancel noted in the fine story he wrote of his trip, it was the last year of legal hunting for the species in Mexico, till the recent limited reopening some 30 years later. The perils and hardships of our trip came mostly from the poor timing, for which we had no choice before classes began.

These mountains were mostly composed of crumbling volcanic rock, dangerous to rely on when climbing. Great chunks would come off in our hands where we sought a purchase. One day Jack and I stood on a rocky mountainside bench, curiously noting a three-foot wide, white strip of limestone, a monolith embedded in the once-liquid lava that dropped steeply some 30 feet to a lower level. Centuries of drainage had worn a polished trough down its length, and the red rock around it had crumbled away, leaving a perfect, elevated, 45 degree angled chute. Not realizing how slick it was, I was nonchalantly standing at its head. Suddenly my feet shot forward, and down the chute I started, scope-sighted rifle slung on one shoulder, canteen flying on the other. Somehow I managed to keep my feet — no doubt from the Minnesota aquaplaning recently left — and landed intact at the bottom. When we incredibly saw that no casualty had come from such a potential disaster, in our relief Jack and I laughed till we were weak. He gasped that all I'd needed was a stem christie at the bottom with the rifle as a pole to make it a perfect ski run!

One evening, I thought that I had come in with a real prize; a canteen full of crystal-clear water! Parched on the mountainside late that day, I had run onto a deep, dark, vertical crevice with green moss, of all things, protruding from the bottom. Peering curiously into its cool, dim depth I saw a pool of clear water in the bottom. It was the first of anything, but liquefied mud, I'd seen to drink for days, and I joyfully slipped my canteen through the six-inch wide crack to plunge it in to fill. Withdrawing it, I drank copiously, then refilled the canteen in the dark pool to take to camp.

I could hardly wait to share my treat till I walked in, and hurried to pour a white enamel cup full as we all drooled. That was the first of the liquid I had seen in clear light, and upon beholding it illuminated in the white cup, I groaned. Barely visible, thousands of nearly microscopic organisms danced in the water. As Charlie shook his head, I thought of all that I had drunk from the canteen, and weakly poured out my very dubious prize. (Maybe that had something to do with the serious illness, surgery and weeks of hospitalization spent after I got back to Tucson, and missed a year of law school.)

Although there had been some encouraging fresh sheep sign in these red mountains, we were finally down to our last day, and still I'd seen no ram. The heat, bad water and climbing had exhausted us till we had little spirit left, but I knew that I'd hate myself forever if I didn't make that last try.

So, after some packing up, Red and I set out late in the morning for a final day on the mountain. He set a rugged pace, for we had to get over the summit in time to watch the far side. I had to plead for mercy from time to time. One of our worst enemies was the great swarm of tiny gnats that continually engulfed us. We moved, ate, drank, and breathed in an atmosphere composed one-half of gnats. They bothered me most when I was climbing, soaked with perspiration and my hands too occupied to brush them off. Then they got into my ears so badly that I had finally, in desperation, made ear muffs of cloth, with drawstrings around the outside. Despite their incongruity in the desert heat, they helped.

Nearly crazed with the droning swarm all over me, I crept up the burning rocks after Rosario, that red-haired will-o'-the-wisp, deliriously panting dreadful imprecations upon all the insect life of Mexico. Reaching the top, we found a breeze that cleared the swarm, and I regained some breath and composure.

There, the scope of the panorama about us was fascinating. From miles away we could see occasional fluffy cumulus clouds building as they floated over the tawny desert. Then the dark, slanting columns of rain would march along under them, usually evaporating short of the scorching earth.

Red and I worked around the peak then, onto a ridge that ran above a big canyon. We soon picked up some very fresh sheep tracks, running along a bench toward the canyon bottom. Some were made by good-sized rams, and our excitement mounted rapidly.

We had followed them but a few yards when Red clutched my arm and whispered hoarsely, "Mira, mira!" (Look!)

He was pointing across the canyon. Following his arm, I saw a line of six rams moving to our right along the opposite canyon wall! They were heading for a notch in the rim close ahead of them.

Quickly, I slipped my arm through the gun sling and dropped prone. The range looked to be about 275 yards. But as I settled down to pick them up in the 4-power Noske scope, the sheep took alarm. They started running, raced through the cleft and disappeared.

Just as I started to scramble to my feet in chagrin, a magnificent ram, evidently the leader, ran up onto a skyline crag across the canyon. There on that rocky turret he poised, quartering toward us, curling horns lifted high, as he searched for the danger. This was such an absolute storybook climax to end the hunt that I am really embarrassed to tell it, but that's just the way it happened, so help me!

It was the picture and the shot of which every hunter dreams. Now, 50 years and many sheep later, I can still see that poised ram in the hot sunlight. How many dry practice shots had I snapped before the trip at a miniature target of just such a ram!

Automatically, then, the cross hairs settled on the top of his shoulder, the finger squeezed. At the rifle's crash, the ram collapsed and pitched off the cliff dead, struck down by a 150-grain thunderbolt.

Red and I joyfully shouted and embraced, then hurriedly scaled down the canyon walls, and up again to reach our trophy. After the sheep was skinned out, a fiendish trip in the afternoon heat lay before us to get the trophy back to camp. We needed some of the meat badly, too, and cut a loin from the ram. It grieved us to be able to handle no more, but a 40-pound head and cape with the meat, rifle, and canteens was a grueling load in the deadly heat, and we had no way to keep the meat.

The canyon seemed infinitely steeper as we started back. By the time we traversed its steep slopes again, worked back around the mountain and down its crumbling walls, we were both at the point of complete prostration. Our canteens were long dry, but throughout the day I had doggedly clung to a quart can of grapefruit juice.

We reeled to the base of the mountain and collapsed under a sparse greasewood bush. Red seemed as done as I. It was a while before we could collect our senses enough to get the can of juice opened. The thought of its contents was about all that had sustained me going down the mountain. That warm, sticky fluid was the most Olympian nectar ever sipped by man, I know. It revived us enough for the final haul over the desert to camp. There, sheep meat and the elation of success eased our exhaustion.

The trip back to Ajo was made without incident. Jack's hunt is a story of its own, but as we sped over the highway back to Tucson, we marveled at the physical toughening that climbing gives. Going past a small, rugged mountain a couple of thousand feet high, Jack said, "I wish I had one of those in my back yard, just to run over before breakfast every morning!"

CRAIG BODDINGTON OF PASO ROBLES, CALIFORNIA, is the Executive Field Editor for PRIMEDIA Outdoor Group, including *GUNS & AMMO* and Petersen's *HUNTING* magazines, and also appears on The Outdoor Channel as co-host for the exciting new series, Guns & Ammo TV. He is the author of 16 books including **Safari Rifles**, **American Hunting Rifles**, **Search for the Spiral Horn**, **and Where Lions Roar**.

Boddington has been a Professional Member of the Boone and Crockett Club since 1981 and has served 30 years as a Marine Corps Infantry Officer.

Fair Chase in North America
was designed using Bookman Old Style and
Impact fonts.

All chapter text and captions written by
Craig Boddington, Professional Member
of the Boone and Crockett Club.

Book, cover, and dust jacket design by
Julie T. Houk, Director of Publications for the
Boone and Crockett Club.

Wildlife sketches graciously donated to the
Boone and Crockett Club by Ken Carlson, Grant
Creek Studio, P.O. Box 1827, Kerrville, TX 78029
telephone - 830/367-5215

Additional copy editing by Sydney Rimpau,
Bozeman, Montana.

Printed and bound hardcover trade and trade
paperback by Walsworth Publishing,
Marceline, Missouri.

Limited edition binding by Roswell Bookbinding,
Phoenix, Arizona.